'H (

INTERNET CELEBRITY

Understanding Fame
Online

D1628686

SOCIETYNOW

SocietyNow: Short, informed books, explaining why our world is the way it is, now.

The *SocietyNow* series provides readers with a definitive snapshot of the events, phenomena and issues that are defining our 21st century world. Written by leading experts in their fields, and publishing as each subject is being contemplated across the globe, titles in the series offer a thoughtful, concise and rapid response to the major political and economic events and social and cultural trends of our time.

SocietyNow makes the best of academic expertise accessible to a wider audience, to help readers untangle the complexities of each topic and make sense of our world the way it is, now.

The Trump Phenomenon: How the Politics of Populism Won in 2016
Peter Kivisto

Becoming Digital: Towards a Post-Internet Society
Vincent Mosco

Understanding Brexit: Why Britain Voted to Leave the European Union
Graham Taylor

Selfies: Why We Love (and Hate) Them
Katrin Tiidenberg

Kardashian Kulture: How Celebrities Changed Life in the 21st Century
Ellis Cashmore

Poverty in Britain: Causes, Consequences and Myths
Tracy Shildrick

INTERNET CELEBRITY

Understanding Fame Online

BY

CRYSTAL ABIDIN

Jönköping University, Sweden

United Kingdom – North America – Japan – India
Malaysia – China

Emerald Publishing Limited
Howard House, Wagon Lane, Bingley BD16 1WA, UK

First edition 2018

British Library Cataloguing in Publication Data
A catalogue record for this book is available from the British
Library

ISBN: 978-1-78756-079-6 (Paperback)
ISBN: 978-1-78756-076-5 (Online)
ISBN: 978-1-78756-078-9 (Epub)

ISOQAR certified
Management System,
awarded to Emerald
for adherence to
Environmental
standard
ISO 14001:2004.

Certificate Number 1985
ISO 14001

INVESTOR IN PEOPLE

To Carissa:
For growing up with me on the internet,
And growing old with me in my heart.

ACKNOWLEDGEMENTS

I have chanced upon the rare luck of being mentored by some of the most intelligent, generous, and caring academics in my field. While there are too many to name here in this book, I would like to thank especially Theresa M. Senft for being an ever critical and mentoring intellectual champion of my research as I build on her milestone work on microcelebrity.

Special thanks to my colleagues Annette Markham and Katrin Tiidenberg who first suggested that I write this book one glorious evening in July 2017, as we lounged over fancy, home-cooked feasts on the coziest rooftop in Aarhus.

Portions of this work were presented at various conferences and seminars, during which I have had the opportunity to field thought-provoking Q&As. While there have been several such events, I would like especially to thank the organizers and attendees of the Affective Politics of Social Media conference at the University of Turku; the Association of Internet Researchers conference 2017 in Tartu; the Australian and New Zealand Communication Association conference 2017 at the University of Sydney; the Centre for Culture and Technology (CCAT) seminar series at Curtin University; the Digitizing Early Childhood International Conference in Perth; and the Digital Living Summer School Programme at Aarhus University.

I wrote this text in the months during which I was a Post-doctoral Fellow at the Media Management and Transformation Centre (MMTC) at Jönköping University, and Adjunct

Research Fellow at the Centre for Culture and Technology (CCAT) at Curtin University. I am grateful for the support and care of my colleagues at both institutions and would like to thank Leona Achtenhagen, Ingrid Aronsson, Barbara Eklöf, Mart Ots, and Emilia Florin Samuelsson from the MMTC, and Emma de Francisco, John Hartley, Tama Leaver, and Lucy Montgomery from the CCAT.

At Emerald Publishing, I am indebted to Jen McCall who first commissioned this text, Rachel Ward for managing the tiresome administrative work, and Sarah Broadley for expertly laboring over marketing the book. I thank also the anonymous reviewers for giving their critical feedback on my work, and the leading scholars in celebrity studies who have generously provided expert blurbs.

The beautiful line sketches were provided by LIBA Studio, to whom I express my admiration of their creativity and my gratitude for their expertise. I would also like to acknowledge Jill Walker Rettberg from whom I adapted this innovative imaging method.

Several ideas and case studies throughout the book were adapted from posts on my academic blog wishcrys.com, on which I write about developments in the world of internet celebrities and vernacular social media cultures. For this, I am thankful to anyone who has ever read, shared, or commented on my running streams of consciousness (affectionately known as 'brainfarts' to my readers) on any of my blogs since 2008.

On social media, I crowdsourced examples of everyone's favorite internet snippet, artifact, icon, or personality to consider a cultural variety of case studies for this book. Thank you to everyone who responded to me. It was a wild experience learning about your guilty pleasures on the internet \ (o ^ ▽ ^ o) ∕.

To some of my most favorite peers in my work life: Kath Albury, Megan Lindsay Brown, Paul Byron, Jocelyn Cleghorn, Stefanie Duguay, Sara Ekberg, Natalie Hendry, Tim Highfield, Jenny Kennedy, Liew Kai Khiun, Maki Mayer, Kristian Møller,

Natalie Pang, Brady Robards, Gabriele de Seta, Sander Schwartz, Tan Shao Han, Katrin Tiidenberg, Son Vivienne, Katie Warfield, and Meg Zeng, thank you for nourishing academia (and my life) with your hearts and your brains ⊂(´• ω •`⊂).

To my people at home: Char+Nick, Jo+Jon, Wei+Joe, thank you for growing old with me <3.

To my person, Sherm: Thank you for being such a wonderfully weird human being. May we ever be blessed with high-speed internet in our home.

And finally, to you, the reader: Thank you for picking up this book. Happy rabbit-holing. Long live the internet.

CONTENTS

LIST OF ILLUSTRATIONS

TABLES

FIGURES

PREFACE

It has been ten years since the first scholarly book on celebrity on the internet was published. Global studies scholar Theresa Senft's *Camgirls* (2008) was a groundbreaking ethnography that traced the practices of young American women who acquired internet fame by broadcasting their personal lives via webcams in their bedrooms. Since then, the structure, nature, and culture of internet celebrity has evolved drastically around the world.

As digital technology has advanced, and social media platforms have instituted new forms of interpersonal communication, internet fame appears to have become increasingly accessible and practiced by or bestowed upon ordinary people from all walks of life. In tandem with this, developments among traditional celebrities and public figures, such as the proliferation of traditional Hollywood-esque celebrities turning to social media to communicate with fans, or politicians taking to social media to cultivate a willing citizenry, also evidence the enduring importance of social media as a mainstream communication tool. Further, amidst the rush for legacy media to move into digital estates to wrestle against their dwindling print media readership, and the rise of the gig economy in which young people are turning to web-based publishing and self-curated content for an income, newer forms of internet celebrity are entangling with and innovating away from older media formats.

In response, this book presents an updated, bird's-eye view of what contemporary internet celebrity and fame online look like. Case studies survey how internet fame is facilitated by the most popular English-language social media platforms today, such as Facebook, Instagram, Reddit, Tumblr, Twitter, and YouTube. However, given that much of the academic research on celebrity culture has thus far been focused on the Global North, and drawing on my research focus on East Asian internet cultures, the case studies discussed were intentionally sampled to include key examples from China, Japan, Singapore, South Korea, and Taiwan, alongside examples from Australia, England, Sweden, and the USA.

A brief note on terminology: While there exists decades of research into the evolution of media industries, from the earliest days of broadcast radio and television, to cross-media formats such as newspapers and print magazines, to contemporary digital formats such as websites and social media, throughout this book I use "traditional media" as a shorthand for these legacy media formats that are generally highly institutionalized, gatekept, hierarchical, and authoritative in the production and circulation of content, as opposed to the more accessible, reciprocal, interactive, open, and democratic uses of "social media."

The accessible language and diverse array of case studies in this book cater to a variety of readers. Students and scholars will find the review of current literature and concepts useful; keen followers of the Influencer scene and people who work in the industry will enjoy the spread of key issues highlighted for discussion; and casual readers who might just like to learn a bit more about internet celebrity will understand how this culture has impacted our contemporary society.

It is my hope that everyone who picks up this book will acquire a valuable insight into internet celebrity culture, beyond the populist claim that these are merely frivolous, vain, or meaningless practices on the internet. Indeed, one of my key scholarly ethics is the belief in "subversive frivolity," wherein practices or objects that are usually brushed off or discarded as marginal, inconsequential, and unproductive hold generative power that is underestimated and under-visibilized because they thrive just under the radar.

In fact, while the notions of "internet" and "celebrity" may immediately bring to mind visualizations of being loud and proud, the impacts of internet celebrity culture are often counterintuitively taking root deeply, slowly but surely, and in quiet confidence, in all aspects of society such as economics, legality, culture, and social issues. As cultures of internet celebrity continue to bloom around the world, the ideas and frameworks in this book will provide provocations and insights for understanding how fame is generated, circulated, sustained, consumed, or rejected on the internet on a global scale.

Finally, a humble request: If you have enjoyed this book, I would love to hear from you. It is always an anxious exercise putting ideas into words, words onto paper, and paper into book form for the world to see. It would be a romantic experiment to watch this little book roam across places akin to the folklore of the traveling garden gnome, so please allow me to trace this journey through digital postcards, i.e. photographs of this text "in the wild." Are you a curious passerby reading it from the comfort of a cosy couch? Are you a student reading it for a class? Are you an internet celebrity reading it between social media updates? Send me photographs from where you are reading this book (plus points for selfies); drop me a message about what you felt (I'm not difficult to locate on the internet); and enchant me with stories about your favorite internet celebrities and artifacts from your part of the world (links!) – I would love to learn more about the quirky rabbit hole of internet celebrity from your part of the internet.

Alternatively, feel free to drop me falling penguin GIFs, Pusheen stickers, or videos of babies tasting lemons for the first time, now that you know where I live on the internet.

Yours,
Crystal Abidin aka wishcrys.

1

WHAT IS AN INTERNET CELEBRITY ANYWAY?

In the 2010s, dominant press coverage and conversations around internet celebrity have focused on just one particular type of celebrity: The Influencer. Influencers are the epitome of internet celebrities, given that they make a living from being celebrities native to and on the internet. Several news reports have been celebrating the success and promise of young Influencers, such as Australian Troye Sivan whose home videos on YouTube eventually grew into a singing contract with EMI Australia, an acting career in Hollywood, and being named by *Time Magazine* as one of the world's 25 most influential teenagers of 2014. Still other reports focus on the shortcomings and scandals of the relatively new Influencer industry, such as when British YouTuber Zoe Sugg, who broke records for being the fastest selling debut novelist, shifting over 78,000 copies in a week in 2014, was exposed for having used a ghostwriter. But internet celebrity is a far broader concept with a much longer history than that of Influencers.

A BRIEF HISTORY OF INTERNET CELEBRITY

There are many theoretical and vernacular accounts of the history of internet fame. But how internet celebrity has come to emerge in various parts of the world varies, depending on the cultural norms of the people, the social practices around media devices and personalities, and the structure of technological capabilities that mediate a population's access to content. While every effort has been made to consider the diverse cultural variety of internet celebrity around the globe, through in-depth case studies throughout the book, this section focuses on a brief history of internet celebrity that happens to be primarily Anglocentric. This is a result of key scholarship in celebrity studies having been published in the English language and focused on media formats that have been popularized in North American, the United Kingdom, and Australia. As such, the conversation does not comprehensively cover the various cultural and platformed histories of internet celebrities.

For instance, the system of celebrity media in Japan distinguishes "mainstream celebrities" in the traditional media industries, such as actors, musicians, and models, from "idols" who are systemically manufactured to serve as cute icons and role models, and from "*tarento*" (タレント) who are recurring personalities on various media and are literally "famous for being famous" without having any other attributes of the entertainment industry. This means that the broad English translation of "internet celebrity" cannot accurately account for the historical, structural, and cultural nuances of distinct types of celebrity in Japan alone. In another instance, in China the vernacular term for internet celebrities is "*wanghong*" (网红), which translates to "red on the internet" with the color red signifying popularity, and broadly refers to highly prolific internet users who are effective conduits for channeling online retail businesses or social media advertising. In other words, these users are assigned celebrity status not for any variety of demonstrable talent, but for their specific ability to attract attention on the internet within the vast ecology of Chinese users. Unlike the connotations of being a "content creator" in the Anglocentric parts of the world, a *wanghong* is premised on the acute ability to convert internet viewer traffic to money, relying less on content production than the ability to hold an audience's attention visually. This means that even where the brushstrokes of internet celebrity translations may heed to some cultural specificities, the benchmark and characteristics of being an internet celebrity can also vary drastically across ecologies. As such, given that it is impossible to provide a comprehensive overview of the *cultural* and *structural* histories of internet celebrity around the world, this section will instead focus on a *theoretical* history of internet celebrity. Giving a brief overview of some of the most important scholarship on celebrity culture, we will go through key ideas that have informed the emergence of celebrities in the age of the internet.

Traditional Celebrities

For most people, the mere mention of the word "celebrity" invokes a visual image of a glamorous Hollywood actor, probably strutting down the red carpet at award ceremonies. Or perhaps you imagine a pop singer performing live on stage to thousands of enthusiastic fans raving in a mosh pit. For others, celebrities can also be internationally known public figures who are prolific for their social status, such as the former President of the USA Barack Obama. Regardless, in the traditional or legacy media industries of cinema, television, radio, music, and print, we have tended to associate the idea of celebrity to an achievement, talent, or position. But being a celebrity in the sense of having fame or being well known is not always tied to these rational and tangible sources.

Research by eminent celebrity studies scholar Graeme Turner[1] shows us that even if some celebrities are first parachuted into the limelight through their achievements, talents, or positions, many of them continue to attract public attention for durations way past the initial instigation, even if they do not continue to commit to or demonstrate their initial sources of fame. This occurs, for instance, when the media starts to report on the private lives of cinema and television actors, musicians, or politicians, even if these affairs are not directly connected to the skills or positions that first made them publicly famous.[2] Considering this, Turner[3] argues that when the public begins to take an interest in a person for their personal lives and identities per se, rather than for what they have done, they are no longer merely public figures but have become bona fide celebrities with public personae. This tells us that although celebrity is traditionally thought of as an innate quality gifted to extraordinary people, contemporary celebrity culture has shifted to focus on people and things that are usually constructed, can be transient, are usually sensational, and often visually based, in tandem with tabloid culture. In other words, the quality of celebrity does not naturally attach to or arise from specific people but is constructed through a process.[4]

The construction of celebrity is supported by intentional media coverage on a person, that turns them into a commodity, where the public is massaged to take interest in them continually. Cultural studies scholars like Chris Rojek[5] have also theorized about celebrity and fame as products of the mass media that specifically highlight a person, attribute special qualities to them, and frame them as being worthy of our attention. Scholars who have studied the industry of creating celebrities have found that it is a networked business comprising entertainment, communications, publicity, representation, appearance, coaching, and endorsement specialists,[6] and it is facilitated with specialized jobs such as managers, agents, publicists, promoters, and magazine editors.[7]

Ordinary People as Celebrities

Since celebrities can be groomed by experts in the traditional media industry, logically speaking, any ordinary, everyday person can be groomed into celebritydom irrespective of whether they have extraordinary achievements, talented skills, or prominent positions in society. As media formats evolved and television genres diversified, ordinary people were increasingly attaining flash fame as guests on talk shows. Specifically, confessional formats like *The Jerry Springer Show* and intervention formats like *Dr. Phil,* where ordinary people are thrust into the spotlight to have their private lives and personal issues turned into public spectacles and commercial subjects, saw the proliferation of fame being attached to the "lived experience of 'the ordinary' "[8], which Turner terms the "demotic turn."

However, what is an "ordinary" life anyway? Sociologist of popular culture Laura Grindstaff[9] contends that "ordinary" does not signpost content as being "average," "typical," or "representative of the population in general," but rather merely conveys that they are not experts or celebrities and are famous for assorted reasons. This includes having firsthand experience of a significant incident or being willing to divulge something attention-worthy from their private lives. Furthermore, as ordinary people are less filtered and orchestrated than traditional celebrities who have been trained in deportment and impression management, it is expected that ordinary people on television are more likely to display intense human emotions in response to specific incidents. This is a moment that Grindstaff[10] terms "the money shot." These highly lifelike displays of emotions range across the spectrum, from happiness and grief to anger and regret, and the audience's ability to identify with these emotions on-screen contributes to feelings that ordinary celebrities are more real and authentic than traditional celebrities.

However, just because there has been an increasing presence of ordinary lives on display does not mean that any ordinary person can be famous for merely publicizing their everyday lives. Fame only attaches to particular forms of everyday life that captivate an audience. Thus, despite the demotic turn, the traditional celebrity industry is not necessarily more democratic because not everyone has an equal opportunity to attain fame[11]. Ultimately, the television industry, like all media industries, relies on public interest and viewership for sustainability, and what attracts attention is entertainment value. In the demotic turn, seemingly authentic and dedicated representations of everyday life "as lived" are but a calculated production of entertainment in the guise of democratic access, and celebrity in the traditional media industries remains hierarchical, exclusive, and gatekept.[12]

Therefore, are there any benefits to the rise of ordinary people and their lives being broadcast on traditional media formats as new forms of celebrity? Scholars argue that there may be several useful outcomes. Broadcasting and celebritizing ordinary lives in traditional media allow viewers to learn and critically assess what is real and what is constructed in the media.[13] It can teach viewers to self-brand[14] and can persuade viewers to practice more reflection and empathy by identifying with other people's stories in a practice that visual media scholar Craig Batty[15] has called "emotioneering." However, despite these apparent benefits, putting ordinary people and their lives on display to reap commercial profits for television stations in exchange for short-lived fame is not a fair game. Such commodification of private lives disproportionately benefits producers and traditional media.

Reality TV Celebrities

As ordinary people and their ordinary lives become increasingly proliferated and lucrative in the traditional media industry, the genre that profits the most from this demotic turn is reality TV. Media scholar Annette Hill[16] writes that reality TV is a form of "popular factual television" where real people perform in (at least) partially staged settings. However, viewers are not passively absorbing and accepting reality TV content just because of its promise of legitimacy derived from having ordinary people as actors. Instead, they hold the expectation that reality TV programming involves a degree of dramatization, sensationalism, and editing of actual experiences, in exchange for being more entertaining. In other words, Hill argues that viewers engage in different forms of viewing strategies to gauge the authenticity of these narratives against their contextual knowledge that popular factual television is particularly performative. Some audiences are more critical toward the truth claims of such programs, while others rely on the belief that all artifice will eventually be exposed.

But what is so special about the format of reality television? Will reality cinema bear the same fruits and expectations? Media scholars Laurie Ouellette and James Hay[17] argue that as a medium, television is "more in sync with the rhythms of everyday life than other media," especially since it is a constantly accessible and consistent mode of entertainment that is available for both "casual observation" and "appointment viewing." As such, television has more power to normalize some social practices and identities as being more accessible, common, and traditional. It is for this reason that the products and services embedded into reality TV programs, especially those of the body makeover genre, tend to be more persuasive forms of advertising for the viewer, since they blur the boundaries between what is merely entertaining content and what is a commercial message.

Celebrity–Audience Relations

In the earlier sections, we learnt that celebrities do not exist as a matter of fact but are constructed through strategic practices, often with the help of expertise from the traditional media industry. We also learnt that both traditional celebrities and ordinary celebrities on talk shows and reality TV have some sort of captivating power that secures the attention and interest of an audience, at least for a period of time. Clearly, there are relationships being fostered between celebrities and their audiences.

One of the most studied relationships between celebrities and their audiences is that of "parasocial relations," a concept cultivated by psychologists Donald Horton and R.Richard Wohl[18] to describe how popular characters on television and radio can instigate the development of one-sided interpersonal relationships with individual members of their audience based on an illusion of intimacy. In the early days of mass media formats, pre-internet and pre-social media, these feelings of intimacy were fostered through television and radio hosts' informal conversational styles of casualness and responsive small talk, the projection of supporting cast members as close friends, mingling with the audience, and the use of technical devices such as close-ups or voice control to appear more friendly, close, and intimate with audiences. The result of such broadcasts is that the audience accumulates extensive knowledge of the television or radio personality, feels as if they are intimate friends, and continues to invest in following their media productions.

Yet the audience never actually experiences any reciprocity from the hosts, who know nothing of their idiosyncrasies. In other words, communication and content only flow from the traditional media hosts to their audience, and there is little opportunity for the latter to respond or personally interact with their hosts across the communication barrier. To understand these mediated forms of intimacy better, Rojek[19] differentiates between "first order intimacy" where feelings of closeness are cultivated through direct meetings and first-hand experiences, and "second order intimacy" where feelings of closeness are artificially stimulated by techniques of the mass media. However, these celebrity–audience relations have changed drastically in the age of digital media.

DIY Celebrity

In tandem with the increasing use of digital technology and social media platforms as sites for circulating personal content, users—whether celebrities, celebrity-wannabes, or audiences—were able to bypass typical corporate layers and structures previously pertinent to manufacturing fame and celebrity. The ability to produce and post "homemade content," so to speak, and the likelihood of this content circulating widely on the internet, independent of the traditional media industries ushered in a new form of ordinary person celebrity that Turner[20] calls the "DIY celebrity." With the new democratizing tools of digital media, celebrity aspirants could earn public attention by publicizing themselves to various interest communities. The DIY celebrity template was comprehensible to and approachable for everyday users with little technical knowledge about attaining fame, because all that they had to do was emulate traditional modes of celebrity production in social media-based adaptations.

Focusing specifically on this new ability for internet users to self-brand and learn to promote themselves to a public, new media scholar P. David Marshall[21] identifies a transition from "representational" to "presentational" media and culture. Before the age of digital media and self-curated content, users could only hope to have their identities and cultures characterized by traditional media actors in broadcast media as "representations." In the age of digital media and DIY content, users are now able to broadcast, control, and negotiate how they would like their identities and cultures to be perceived as intentional "presentations" of the self.

As self-presentation on digital media became more accessible, professor of television and digital culture James Bennett[22] observed that such DIY celebrities and aspirants increasingly pursued fame that more resembled the old-school, traditional media models of celebrity, based on achievements, skills, or positions as discussed earlier. The chief implication of this is that despite the new possibilities and promises of emerging types of celebrity in the age of digital media, many DIY celebrities still tended to borrow from the practices of traditional entertainment industries.[23] As a result, several digital media scholars—such as Jean Burgess and Joshua Green who studied early YouTube culture,[24] and Alice Marwick and danah boyd who studied celebrity culture on Twitter[25]—have argued that ordinary people's success at attaining fame and celebrity still becomes subject to the benchmarks and logics of traditional media. In the earliest days of Web 2.0, blogs were the primary platform on which DIY celebrities on the internet could fashion themselves. However, when webcams became popular for everyday use in the late 1990s, the era of "camgirls" that mirrored reality TV celebrities ushered in a new form of celebrity.

Microcelebrity

One of the earliest extended academic studies of bedroom webcamming behavior was conducted by global studies scholar Theresa Senft,[26] who investigated a generation of camgirls and their audiences between 2000 and 2004. These camgirls were knowingly broadcasting themselves to the public on the internet while attempting to accumulate fame. Senft describes this form of celebrity pursuit as "micro-celebrity," where users employ digital media technologies and platforms to garner popularity by performing on the internet.[27] Their main strategies include cultivating a public image of themselves as a brand and interacting with viewers through emotional labor.[28]

Using camgirls as a vehicle for understanding this new form of celebrity, Senft argued that microcelebrities on the internet were unlike celebrities in the traditional entertainment industries on several counts[29]—where traditional celebrities practice a sense of separation and distance from their audiences, microcelebrities have their popularity premised on feelings of connection and interactive responsiveness with their audiences; where traditional celebrities may be known for their performance craft and skills, microcelebrities are expected to display themselves unedited as "real" people with "real" issues; and where traditional celebrities may have extensive fame among a large global audience, microcelebrities exercise a popularity that while narrower in breadth is far deeper. Further, microcelebrities hold a stronger obligation to their audiences than traditional celebrities, as the fame of the former is co-constructed through a community of interested viewers on the internet rather than by the mere mechanisms of the traditional entertainment industry.

While Senft introduced the concept of microcelebrity through camgirls who videocammed as a hobby, the theory of microcelebrity was further developed through a second major study conducted by communication scholar Alice Marwick[30] who studied San Francisco tech industry workers using social media as a networking tool in the early 2000s. Marwick argues that for microcelebrity to be successfully enacted, performers must curate a persona that continuously feels authentic, interactive, and celebrity-like regardless of the size or state of one's audience.[31] This perpetual livestream of the branded self requires the cultivation of a mindset that all friends and followers on the internet are prospective audiences and fans,[32] which Marwick asserts, drawing upon the work by Rojek, can result in two forms of microcelebrity. Where "ascribed" microcelebrities must constantly posit themselves as being of a higher status than their followers to garner celebrity treatment,[33] "achieved" microcelebrities build their fame by selectively revealing confidential information to viewers to cultivate feelings of intimacy with them.[34]

Studies in microcelebrity have since expanded across various demographics of internet users. For instance, microcelebrity has been theorized as labor,[35,36,37] branding,[38] and linguistic practice.[39] It has been practiced among academics,[40] activists,[41] and professional gamers and artists,[42] and in specific cultural locales outside of the dominant Anglocentric, English-speaking, Global North platforms such as China[43,44] and Indonesia.[45] The ways that researchers have been thinking about microcelebrity have also been progressing. Instead of focusing only on specific practices or groups of people, more studies are looking at community norms among specific types of microcelebrities,[46] whether each social media platform tends to promote its own set of preferred practices among users,[47] and how the value of celebrity can be dispersed across different platforms.[48]

However, in the ten years since microcelebrity studies were first launched, social media platforms, internet norms, and the sociocultural uses and impacts of generating celebrity on the internet have developed rapidly. In the U.S., microcelebrities may have begun as hobbyists[49] and adapted into networkers with professional businesses.[50] In other parts of the world, like Singapore, they began as home-based fashion entrepreneurs through a makeshift online sales format known as "blogshops".[51] But today, being a microcelebrity has become a full-time vocational job for some as Influencers (see Chapter 4). Moreover, this era of the most commercialized form of microcelebrity has ushered in a variety of internet celebrity innovations. For instance, as an anthropologist, I have studied how Influencers who were the earliest adopters of social media regularly subvert the intended uses of apps like Instagram by strategizing their content into a commercial endeavor, [52, 53]often at the expense of the free labor offered by their loyal followers.[54] Further, as the earliest cohorts of Influencers progress in their lives to become romantic partners and parents, many of them are also grooming and growing (literally) their children into second-generation microcelebrities known as "micro-microcelebrities",[55] while other ordinary families are becoming internet celebrities by branding themselves as "family Influencers".[56] These structural shifts in microcelebrity thus warrant a new theorizing for a broader, more comprehensive theory of internet celebrity.

Internet celebrity

From fashion Instagrammers in Australia, YouTube gamers in Sweden, and beauty bloggers in the UK, to *mukbang* eaters in South Korea, *zhibowanghong* in China, and parody Tweeters in India, the face of internet celebrity is rapidly diversifying and evolving. Different forms of internet celebrity have emerged in the last decade, such as memes, transient virality, trending social media posts, accidental celebrity from controversy and bad publicity, and intentional self-branded social media influencers. Digital culture on social media, and celebrity culture on traditional media are also weaving into each other, such that breakout stars from one-hit viral videos can parlay their transient fame into a full-time career, while ailing legacy media formats learn to capitalize upon vernacular participatory cultures to sustain their businesses. But what has changed between the era of microcelebrity and the current climate of internet celebrity?

With a basic knowledge of how social media platforms work, anyone has the potential to become a microcelebrity, but not everyone may successfully groom their microcelebrity into a vocation like Influencers, or on the scale of internet celebrities. As the in-depth case studies in the later chapters will evidence, internet celebrities can be assessed based on six measures:

(1) Whereas the *scale* of microcelebrities used to be small and positioned in opposition to traditional celebrities of the entertainment industry, today it is not uncommon for internet celebrities to rival or surpass traditional celebrities in terms of global popularity or reach;

(2) Whereas the *platform* of microcelebrities used to be confined to internet technologies such as webcams, or social media such as Twitter, internet celebrities are increasingly crossing between various estates on social

and traditional media platforms to maintain their
following[57];

(3) Whereas the *audiences* of microcelebrities used to be
     a niche of dedicated internet users, internet users are
     building audiences on a global scale made up of loyal
     followers, casual viewers, and chance watchers alike
     with the help of social media algorithms and traditional
     media mechanisms that intentionally amplify some
     forms of internet celebrity (see Chapter 3);

(4) Whereas the *nature* of microcelebrities used to be premised
     as a hobby or a complementary networking tool to support
     a formal business endeavor, many internet celebrities are
     presently pursuing fame professionally as a vocation;

(5) Whereas the *practice* of microcelebrity used to depend
     largely on interactive intimacies and selective disclosure
     of privacy, internet celebrities are fronting both
     "anchor" thematic content in which they demonstrate
     their talents and skills, and "filler" emotional content in
     which they display snippets of everyday life to maintain
     a sense of ordinariness[58]; and

(6) Whereas the *impact* of microcelebrities used to be confined
     to the bedroom for identity-making or in the locale of an
     office for networking purposes, internet celebrities are
     making waves from blogsites in bedrooms to broadcasts
     on traditional media, and even setting up sizable
     businesses where they wield influence in boardrooms.

Now that we have established the architecture of internet celebrity and the extent of their fame, we can turn to establish what
an internet celebrity really is. Internet celebrity refers to all
media formats (people, products, icons, figures, etc.) that attain
prominence and popularity native to the internet, although the

Table 1.1.   Structural differences between microcelebrity and internet celebrity

Factor	Microcelebrity	Internet celebrity
Scale	Opposing traditional media	Exceeding traditional media
Platform	Internet, social media	Multi-platform, social and traditional media
Audience	Niche, online	Global, online and offline
Nature	Hobby, networking	By chance, hobby, networking, vocation
Practice	Disclosure	Anchor talents/skills, filler everyday life
Impact	Bedrooms	Boardrooms

spillover effects and afterlives may include cross-border flows outside of the internet. Internet celebrities are mainly known for their high visibility, whether this be attributed to fame or infamy, positive or negative attention, talent and skill or otherwise, and whether it be sustained or transient, intentional or by happenstance, monetized or not. More crucially, internet celebrity has to be received, watched, and acknowledged by an audience—someone who expends great effort to put out quality content on the internet but is not watched and validated by anyone will not become an internet celebrity. As such, the success and extent of an internet celebrity's high visibility can vary depending on the platforms they use and the cultural ideologies and tastes of their intended audience.

What about traditional celebrities on the internet?

As internet celebrities accumulate extensive fame across social and traditional media platforms, and as the use of social media becomes more mainstream among bona fide celebrities from the traditional entertainment industries, it is sometimes difficult to distinguish between internet(-native) celebrities and (traditional) celebrities on the internet. After all, traditional celebrities are increasingly duplicating their content from traditional media to social media to engage with a wider (and often younger) audience.

British talk show host James Corden runs a popular segment on television in which he carpools and sings with notable musicians.[59] These clips are then uploaded onto YouTube, where his videos often go viral. Armenian-American reality TV family, the Kardashian-Jenners, profit from social media through sponsored advertisements; they use the internet to promote their cosmetic and fashion brands and selectively post self-branded content to catch their followers' attention in a feedback loop that channels viewership back to their traditional media estates.[60] Black American Hollywood actress Chrissy Teigen is prolific for live-tweeting about her personal life and marriage to singer-songwriter John Legend, breaking down the long-established boundaries and distance between fans and traditional celebrities, and even calling upon social media followers for highly documented personal favors.[61] But public figures outside the entertainment industry are doing it too. Singaporean Member of Parliament Baey Yam Keng has been branded by the press as a "selfie king" for using his highly curated Instagram selfies to engage with his younger populace,[62] and French presidential candidates in the 2017 elections have used Snapchat and its comedic filters to portray a lighter side of their public personae while campaigning.[63]

Although these traditional celebrities and public figures are adopting social media strategies originally generated by internet celebrities to reach a wider audience, we are reminded by scholars like Marwick[64] that the self-preservation strategies and defensive structures at the disposal of the former are not always available to the latter, and by scholars like Senft[65] that internet fame that was co-constructed with a watchful

audience remains dependent and vulnerable to their prefer-
ences. Furthermore, where traditional celebrities and public
figures generally acquire fame for their achievements, talents,
or positions, and where their private lives are subject to the
shadow economy of tabloid media, internet celebrities who
choose to hone their public fame are continually required to
indulge in greater disclosures of the self to maintain follower
interest as the market becomes saturated.

CONCLUSION

In this chapter, we reviewed a theoretical history of internet
celebrities, tracing how they have evolved from older celebrity formats, including traditional celebrities, ordinary people
as celebrities, reality TV celebrities, celebrity–audience relations, DIY celebrities, and microcelebrities. We also discussed
how traditional celebrities are increasingly borrowing from
the strategies of internet celebrities in their self-branding on
social media. In the next chapter, we transit from theoretical
histories to performative cultures of internet celebrity, focusing on their four main qualities in relation to forms of capital
and value.

2

QUALITIES OF INTERNET CELEBRITY

Internet celebrity is a product of performance and perception. It can be generated when intentionally "performed" by an entity (whether person, animal, or non-living object), or may arise when unwittingly "perceived" by an audience to have the quality of internet celebritydom. While there are several factors that define a text or performance as having fame or infamy, most often internet celebrities are given attention and celebrated for their exclusivity, exoticism, exceptionalism, or everydayness (see Chapter 1 for theoretical inspirations behind these categories). However, what is it that makes these four qualities so special?

A noted French sociologist Pierre Bourdieu created a framework to understand forms of "capital" in order to explain how society comes to exercise judgments in taste, express aesthetic dispositions, and assign status and distinction towards different social behaviors.[66] The qualities of exclusivity, exoticism, exceptionalism, and everydayness, each corresponds to a specific form of capital that arouse interest and attention, whether positive (i.e., out of admiration or love) or negative (i.e., out of disgust or judgment).

Just as social, cultural, and technical forms overlap and are partly derived from economic capital, the qualities of internet celebrity are not clear-cut. A combination of each of these qualities may exist in any instance of internet celebrity, but this chapter will focus on specific case studies that best illustrate the core of these qualities when successfully enacted.

EXCLUSIVITY

Internet celebrity that is "exclusive" is the glamorization and celebration of practices and possessions so elite in access or rare in occurrence that it would be unusual for ordinary people to experience them without high "economic capital." Economic capital refers to the assets that are monetary or have monetary value attached to them and can thus be directly converted into money from their institutionalized forms, such as property and goods.[67]

The phenomenon of "The Rich Kids of Instagram" is a classic example of exclusive internet celebrity that is dependent on economic capital. In popular discourse, it usually acronymizes as "RKOI" and generally denotes teens and young adults who conspicuously display their opulent lifestyles through material possessions and extravagant experiences, such as owning a fleet of luxury cars, excessively engaging in fine dining, or frequently traveling on business class flights. In so doing, they attract massive amounts of attention from social media followers through "follows" and "likes" and are bestowed with publicity, acclamation, or in some cases infamy.

The phrase "RKOI" debuted and was popularized in July 2012 after an anonymous blogger started the Tumblr account richkidsofinstagram.tumblr.com – later migrating to therkoi.com – to repost Instagram photographs and their original captions from young wealthy users dubbed "the 1%." These RKOI images were easily searchable as users usually hashtagged their posts with consciously exclusive keywords such as "#wealth," "#mansion," and "#yacht".[68] The anonymous blogger later launched a companion Instagram account @rkoi to cross-post images from its Tumblr, with an account biography that succinctly informs viewers that the images depict what the RKOI, who have more money than the average person, do in their private lives. At the time of writing, the account has over 417,000 followers[69] and has been headlined and featured in hundreds of news articles around the world.

So ubiquitous is the RKOI genre of exclusive internet celebrity that spin-off accounts featuring local internet celebrities have proliferated internationally in wealthy capitals such as Dubai,[70] Hong Kong,[71] and Switzerland,[72] and even in countries with traditionally lower gross domestic products (GDPs),

Figure 2.1.   Artist's impression of a typical "Rich Kids of Instagram" post, featuring a woman clad in a bikini lying on a yacht at sea. Art produced by LIBA Studio. Used with permission.

such as Albania[73],Nigeria,[74] and Vietnam.[75] The exclusivity of internet celebrity among the likes of the RKOI have proven to be so alluring that traditional media industries have also begun to produce insights into the phenomenon through paperback novels[76] and reality TV documentaries based on American[77] and British[78] RKOI.

In her interview with a group of RKOI for *Vice*, journalist Chem Squier queries the young and wealthy over their internet celebrity status achieved almost solely by flaunting wealth on the internet. To this, an RKOI internet celebrity pseudonymized as "Luke" replied that it was merely a strategy to provoke and shock viewers, while @akinbelfon17 (Instagram account now defunct) asserted that her primary objective for posting pictures was to become famous.[79] Perhaps the appeal of exclusivity as a route to internet celebrity is best summarized by the account biography by spin-off RKOI account @richkidsof, which crassly states that viewers do not get to see "this shit" on a regular basis.[80]

EXOTICISM

Internet celebrity that is "exotic" is perceived as distancing, far removed from one's comfort zone, or so novel or foreign that it piques the interest of audiences who hold contrasting or different forms of "cultural capital." Cultural capital refers to the embodied, objectified, or institutionalized assets that are accumulated through the cultivation of valued personal qualities, tasteful material objects, credentials, and qualifications.[81]

Given that the forms of cultural capital that are preferred and privileged in society vary across cultures, exotic internet celebrity is thus a result of generative frictions between the celebrity and the viewer. This means that exotic internet celebrity arises whenever there is a gap in what is considered culturally normal or mainstream between the performer's and the audience's backgrounds and can occur within inter- and intracultural settings depending on the nuance of difference.

The distance of this cultural gap between the performer and the audience, and thus the extent of exoticism and celebrity bestowed upon the performer, is highly dependent on the "intersectionality" between the internet celebrity and the audience. Intersectionality is a concept coined by the critical race theorist Kimberlé Crenshaw to describe how the interconnected (and usually minority) identity categories of race and ethnicity, gender and sexuality, and class and status are related to systems of power.[82] As such, depending on the combination of a viewer's identity categories, they may perceive the performance of an internet celebrity as very exotic and attention-worthy or too mundane to warrant any attention.

To understand how exotic internet celebrity arises in inter- and intracultural contexts, we turn as a case study to Kinoshita Yuka, a Japanese competitive eater – a practice better known by its original South Korean name as *mukbang* (먹방) or by its Japanese terminology *oogui* (大食い).

Kinoshita has headlined global news for her viral binge-eating videos that are posted on her YouTube channel,[83] where she speaks in Japanese and English captions are provided. Some of her most notable feats include eating, in one videotaped sitting, 100 hamburgers from McDonald's, 9,102 kcal of Taiwanese beef ramen, or 7 kg of Hello Kitty decorated birthday cake. Kinoshita begins each video by laying out the copious amounts of food she is about to eat in a flat lay. If she makes the meal from scratch, Kinoshita holds up ingredients to the camera while recording the cooking process – boiling, simmering, frying, stirring – highlighting heavy foods such as meat and carbohydrates enveloped in oil bubbles and steam. The sheer amount of raw ingredients she uses is intended to induce shock as viewers get a clear grasp of the amount of calories she will actually consume.

If she purchases ready-made food, Kinoshita preserves the original food packaging for her opening flat lay, laying one food item at a time on her table in a sped-up, fast-forwarded video sequence. With household famous brand logos such as McDonald's and Pizza Hut on display, viewers can identify with the everydayness of the foods Kinoshita binge eats. This awareness solicits a sense of relatability in viewers, inviting them to compare their ordinary capacity of consumption with that of Kinoshita's grotesque intake, as they stare and squirm over stretching the limits of the human body.

Kinoshita draws viewers in with her chirpy commentary, which are addressed to viewers in the first person, while she holds the gaze of the camera/viewers and polishes the foods off in one sitting with no display of discomfort. This is made

Figure 2.2.   Artist's impression of Kinoshita Yuka's typical *mukbang* spread, sitting behind a table full of plates of food. Art produced by LIBA Studio. Used with permission.

even more spectacular as Kinoshita is skinny, young, and gives the impression of frailty through her usual wardrobe of layered tops and cardigans to protect her from the cold – in short, she is the antithesis of the typical *mukbang* eater whom one imagines to be male, brawny, and hardy.

Viewers who first chance upon Kinoshita are always surprised at her feats for several reasons. A selection of comments paraphrased from one of her most popular videos in which she eats 48 pieces of KFC chicken from four buckets evidences this.[84] Often, Kinoshita is gawked at by viewers in awe of the copious amounts she consumes. Sentiments include:

> *I feel sick just watching this.*
>
> *What the heck. I can't believe what I saw.*
>
> *Oh my god. Are you a monster?*

Furthermore, the fact that she is a female *mukbang* eater casts her in an exotic light amidst the male-dominated broadcast scene. Sentiments include,

> *You ate 48 pieces of chicken? And you're a girl?*
>
> *Haha, your eating makes me, a grown man, look weak.*

Among the small subculture of female *mukbang* eaters, Kinoshita is also captivating for her uncharacteristically svelte appearance despite what is perceived to be uncouth binge eating. Sentiments include,

> *Oh! You're so small sized! How did you eat all of that?*
>
> *I don't understand how you are not fat!*
>
> *You're quite cute!*

Finally, Kinoshita's popularity and celebrity are often reduced to the popular YouTube trope of "Asians doing weird shit," as viewers rationalize away her achievements and exoticism as being "just Asian." Sentiments include,

> *This is crazy. It only happens in Asia.*

> *Asians are super human.*

> *Wow Asian girls look so beautiful and delicate that it is pleasing even to watch them down 4 buckets of chicken!*

In each group of comments, the intersectionality of Kinoshita's identity markers is compounded as she is singled out as a *mukbang* eater, a female *mukbang* eater, a slim female *mukbang* eater, and finally a slim Asian female *mukbang* eater, exacerbating her exoticism and the audience's corresponding interest in her. These comments casting Kinoshita in an exotic light are unsurprising and are common in the comments sections for East Asian internet celebrities who have gained traction in Anglocentric places. To comprehend this patterned behavior, we must understand the concepts of "ethnocentrism" and "orientalism."

Ethnocentrism is the judgment of other cultures by the customs and standards of one's own culture, resulting in the belief that other cultures are inferior in standards or values. It is usually also referred to as "Americentrism" or "Eurocentrism" when Americans or Europeans exercise bias towards their own cultures and worldviews and assume the inferiority of others by default. Ethnocentrism is usually mobilized in tandem with orientalism, a concept coined by the postcolonial public intellectual Edward W. Said to describe the prejudices of Western cultures as permeated through romanticized, false, or exaggerated cultural representations of Asia.[85] The YouTube comments that explain away Kinoshita's abilities by

way of her being simply "Asian" are evidence of this orientalism at play, just as how the virality of Japanese entertainer
Pikotaro's parody video "PPAP" (Pen-Pineapple-Apple-Pen)
was almost entirely celebrated for its Asian exoticism in
popular press reports,[86] and how the global uptake of Chinese photo-editing app *Meitu Xiuxiu* was attributed largely
to reveling in the "bizarre" and "alien" spaces of East Asian
internet cultures.[87]

Evidently, in the intercultural space of a global platform
like YouTube, Kinoshita holds exotic internet celebrity. She
is relatively well known and successful despite being from a
minority demographic. Although she boasts over 3.7 million
subscribers and over 1.2 billion views since having begun her
channel in 2014,[88] on YouTube, Kinoshita is still a minority
content creator in terms of gender, genre, and cultural speci-
ficity: A 2015 study conducted by YouTube analytics company OpenSlate indicated that the platform is still dominated by
men in 90% of all the 51 categories of available content, and
that "female-dominated YouTube categories" are feminine
in nature comprising "Makeup & Cosmetics," "Skin & Nail
Care," and "Weight Loss",[89] which are very different from
Kinoshita's *mukbang* genre. Social media marketing company
Socialbakers reports that the top online entertainment show
channels on YouTube are based in the USA and belong to
the genres of gaming and product reviews,[90] unlike Kinoshita's genre of food and challenge videos that are particularly
popular in East Asia. Social media analytics company Social
Blade also reveals that among entertainment genre channels
on YouTube the most viewed videos are in the English language,[91] while Kinoshita's videos are spoken in Japanese and
subtitled in English.

However, even within the intracultural space of Japan and
Japanese internet celebrity, Kinoshita is still characterized by
a degree of exoticism. The clear majority of popular female

YouTubers in Japan belong to the hyperfeminized genre of fashion and beauty. They include top-ranked stars such as "さぁや saaya",[92] "sasakiasahi",[93] and "SekineRisa".[94] Kinoshita's inter- and intracultural exoticism has led hers to being ranked the fourth most subscribed YouTube channel in Japan.[95] But this performance is a rarity considering the fact that the most watched Japanese YouTube channels are regularly in the genres of music, such as label "Universal Music Japan"[96] or girl group "AKB48"[97]; children's activities such as "Kan & Aki's CHANNEL"[98] or "がっちゃんねる★The-Gacchannel"[99] featuring young children playing with toys or going on excursions; and male-hosted entertainment such as "兄者弟者"[100] featuring video gameplay or "HikakinTV"[101] featuring comedic skits and challenges.[102] Kinoshita experiences a double layer of exoticism within inter- and intracultural spaces, and this compounds viewers' interest in her and increases her subsequent internet celebrity.

EXCEPTIONALISM

Internet celebrity that is "exceptional" highlights the unusual abilities, astounding qualities, or expert skills of a person that can be elite or mundane in nature but are spectacular and admired for their "technical capital" all the same. Although Pierre Bourdieu does not define technical capital per se, he discusses it as a derivative and a combination of economic, cultural, and social capital. Contemporary theorists like the social computing scholar Sarita Yardi[103] and disability and education scholar Simon Hayhoe[104] have studied forms of technical capital, which they define as the knowledge and mobilization of digital technologies to access information, achieve social mobility, and ensure social inclusivity. Although traditionally, exceptionalism in performance pertains to the realm of highly specialized skills, the attention economy of the internet is more democratic and embracing of various skill sets, both elite and mundane.

One example of internet celebrity as the celebration of exceptionalism is that of the 21-year-old South Korean musician Sungha Jung. He first became popular on YouTube at the young age of 10 as a guitar prodigy. With a guitar larger than his body and his tiny fingers stretching to reach across the fretboard, Jung's fingerstyle acoustic guitar covers of popular songs requires proficient technical skills beyond that of mainstream guitar-playing techniques. Further, he arranges the covers himself by ear, and his videos have earned him 1.4 billion views and 4.8 million subscribers on YouTube.[105] One of the spikes in

Figure 2.3.   Artist's impression of Sungha Jung playing his guitar on YouTube. Art produced by LIBA Studio. Used with permission.

his online fame is attributed to his cover of the theme from the movie *Pirates of The Caribbean*, which has accumulated over 56 million views at the time of writing.[106] The video caught the attention of renowned guitarists Hata Shuji and Ulli Bögershausen who have offered to become his personal mentors.[107]

Jung has since been able to parlay his YouTube fame into several studio albums,[108] annual concert tours around the world,[109] endorsements by several music brands,[110] and appearances in a documentary on fingerstyle acoustic guitar playing[111]. Given his decade-long presence on YouTube, growing from being a young boy to a young adult, Jung's fans have expressed their pleasure at having been able to witness his skills mature online.[112, 113] In recent years, to keep up with the evolution of social media and to engage with his younger generation of fans, Jung has expanded his internet presence to Instagram where he publishes photographs with fans and renowned musicians, and short video teasers to his full-length YouTube videos.[114]

Although an exceptional internet celebrity like Sungha Jung is celebrated for his elite skills, such exceptionalism can also extend to mundane and everyday skills. In early 2017, a string of videos starring a young Chinese woman using office props as makeshift culinary tools started gaining viral traction on Facebook. Known only by her handle "Ms Yeah," the woman engaged in quirky experiments in the office such as baking a cake in her office drawer with a light bulb and tinfoil or using a fire extinguisher to make ice-cream.[115] Several trend reports quickly uncovered that 23-year-old Zhou Xiao Hui was the star of these "office chef" videos.

Originally from Chengdu in Sichuan province, she is known as "办公室小野" (*ban gong shi xiao ye*) in China, the moniker under which she has been publishing videos since January 2017, where she has over 3.5 million followers on *Weibo*[116] and over 1.3 million followers on the Chinese streaming site *MeiPai*.[117] A month later, Ms Yeah cross-posted her videos onto YouTube where she quickly amassed viewers and fans from around the world.[118] Ms Yeah uploaded new makeshift culinary videos on all platforms at least once a week, and her viral fame on Facebook continued to captivate audiences. At the time of writing, she boasts over 3.2 million followers on Facebook,[119] over 3 billion views across all her cooking videos,[120] and a sustained average of 500,000 to 1 million views per video.[121]

The reasons for Ms Yeah's national and international reach can be attributed to several factors. For one, she and her team intentionally position her videos for cross-cultural reach in the international market, revealing in an interview with *Reuters* that dialogue is minimized such that "everyone watches the video in silence, [and] foodies from all over the world can understand what we are doing".[122] She also uses "universally understood emojis" and subtitles if there is any dialogue at all,[123]

Figure 2.4. Artist's impression of Ms Yeah cooking dishes with office equipment, such as using a blow dryer and coffee pot. Art produced by LIBA Studio. Used with permission.

to give her non-Mandarin-speaking viewers context. More crucially, Ms Yeah's unusual makeshift culinary skills that churn out edible meals demarcate her as exceptionally resourceful and adventurous. Moreover, against the backdrop of "run-of-the-pepper-mill celebrity chef[s] or food blogger[s]",[124] and the usually demure and graceful female entertainers in China's *zhibo wanghong* or livestreaming internet celebrity scene,[125,126] Ms Yeah's mime-like comedy and skillful makeshift culinary skills emerge as especially memorable.

What had begun as her first experimental video to grill beef with an iron is now a full-time project managed by a team of six staff members who produce content for Ms Yeah's platforms.[127] Although in an interview in the early days of her fame in April 2017, Ms Yeah claimed not to be interested in the "commercial requests" that were flooding in, China's internet celebrity industry, valued at around USD8.5 million in 2016,[128] proved too lucrative to ignore. Ms Yeah has since swiftly transited into producing sponsored videos and branded content, including collaborating with Chinese import–export giant Alibaba's Jack Ma.[129] However, she remains reflexive and acknowledges that the boundaries of exceptionalism and incredible skill on the internet are constantly shifting, and that her content will "eventually get boring." As such, she is delicately diversifying her content by venturing into food-related cosmetic videos – such as using tomato juice as lipstick, or marshmallows as a makeup sponge[130] – to solidify her transition from one-hit wonder to sustained internet celebrity.

EVERYDAYNESS

Internet celebrity that is "everyday" curates the usually mundane and ordinary aspects of daily life with such candor and insight (as well as with much regularity and consistency) that a sustained social relationship based on a sense of community and trust is fostered as "social capital." Social capital refers to the assets arising from stable networks of relationships between people, organizations, or institutions, through acknowledged membership within these groups.[131] The sustained and regular interactions of everyday internet celebrities with their audience prime their digital estates as networked spaces for like-minded viewers to congregate and keep up-to-date. Over time, this sense of familiarity and trust allows everyday internet celebrities to promote other persons, products, or services through personal recommendations and endorsements.

The most common instances of everyday internet celebrity include users who post daily "outfits of the day' or "OOTDs," lifestyle or parenting blogs in which users reveal sneak peeks into their daily routines, or the traveling artifact trope, like the classic "traveling garden gnome." At the confluence of all these genres is "Naptime With Joey" – a pastiche of costume dress-up emulating iconic characters or cosplay, mommy blogging, and travel photography. In early 2016, Los Angeles-based mother and photographer Laura Izumikawa first began dressing up and photographing her four-month-old sleeping infant in various costumes.

On Instagram, Joey Marie Choi cosplays daily during naptime in a vast assortment of costumes, appearing dressed as, for example, a piece of sushi, a barista, Jon Snow from *Game of Thrones*, or the cartoon character Pikachu.[132] The excitement caused by waiting for these daily updates stems, in part, also from Izumikawa's ability to keep up with trends that resonate with her audience, for instance dressing Joey as parody Japanese artist Pikotaro when the catchy tune "PPAP" went viral on YouTube, or as the character Barbara from Netflix's *Stranger Things* when the hashtag "#justice4barb" trended on Twitter.

Figure 2.5. Artist's impression of "Naptime With Joey" in a typical costume. Art produced by LIBA Studio. Used with permission.

As well as building a sense of anticipation around the daily photo update, Naptime With Joey also appeals to followers by using discursive narratives, visual images, and video diaries to project a coherent narrative about the joys and struggles of parenting, and organisational skills around domestic management and family life. Mother Izumikawa explains that she began photographing her daughter to "memorialize her growth and little milestones," and the "little props" she added were intended to create "hilarious pictures" for Joey's grandparents who do not live with them.[133] Over time, Izumikawa explains that the archive of images served as "[m]emories of bonding with Joey and watching her grow bigger and differently every week... the transformation of her growth".[134] Alongside this heartwarming backstory is Izumikawa's altruistic aim for the project to "remind parents to have fun with their kids and not get too caught up in the seriousness of parenting".[135]

Naptime With Joey's fame on Instagram eventually led to a book deal comprising a selection of Joey's photographs with publisher Gallery Books in 2017, after several requests from Instagram followers.[136] Despite Naptime With Joey's continually expanding fame around the globe, the project maintains its flavor of everydayness and humility through an extension of press collateral and personal updates from Izumikawa on her various social media. For instance, she still expresses surprise at Joey's fame despite her successful earnings from book sales and product placements[137]: "My photos of my napping daughter dressed up as pop culture icons became viral one day and now I blog about our lives because it turns out, people want to know more about us which is totally crazy to me!".[138]

At the time of writing, the Naptime With Joey Instagram account boasts over 620,000 followers and features a mix of public relations material – such as book promotions, book tours, sponsored posts, product placements[139] – and domestic revelation material – such as Joey's growth milestones, Joey's mealtimes, the family's celebrations around special occasions, and vlogs of everyday domestic life. Izumikawa now describes herself as a "stay-at-home-working-mom",[140] highlighting her role as a parent over that of the creator of an everyday internet celebrity.

CONCLUSION

In this chapter, we reviewed some key qualities of internet celebrity to understand how different personalities accrue fame on the internet for being exclusive, exotic, exceptional, or everyday. Where exclusive internet celebrity incites voyeurism over the excess of elite materiality, exotic internet celebrity captures attention for being foreign and outside of one's comfort zone. Where exceptional internet celebrity captures audiences for their highly technical skills, everyday internet celebrity generates feelings of affect and connectedness from regularity and consistency. We learnt how these types of internet celebrity engage with forms of economic, cultural, technical, and social capital to attract an audience, as illustrated through the case studies of the Rich Kids of Instagram popularized in Anglo- and Eurocentric contexts, Kinoshita Yuka from Japan, Sungha Jung from South Korea, Ms Yeah from China, and Naptime With Joey who are Asian-Americans. In the next chapter, we will learn about the relationship between internet celebrity and the traditional media industry, including the interdependent relationship between both industries.

3

INTERNET CELEBRITY
AND TRADITIONAL MEDIA

As internet celebrity has proliferated, news coverage and popular discourse on the topic has been on the rise. Yet, the ways in which we conceptualize the rather distinct and nuanced forms of internet celebrity are still simplified, reductive, and obscures the complexity of the phenomenon's impact on society.

In this chapter, you will find a framework within which to think about internet celebrity and its relationship with traditional media via an analysis of five common types of internet celebrity. We focus specifically on how an increasing number of internet celebrity formats derive from, overlap with, and display spillover effects with other media industries in society. This signifies that the rise of the attention economy on digital spaces, championed by social media celebrities, is simultaneously capitalizing on and being cannibalized by legacy media, as both industries compete and cooperate for a digital audience.

The types discussed in this taxonomy and their relationship with legacy media include eyewitness viral stars, meme personalities, spotted and groomed investments, crowd-puller cameos, and weaponized microcelebrity.

EYEWITNESS VIRAL STARS

"Eyewitness viral stars" considers the creation of an accidental and transient form of viral internet celebrity. Such persons
are usually interviewees on television news, many of whom
are victims of the incidents being reported about, who attain
overnight fame through news-reporting strategies and news
network circuits that curate and disseminate their sensational and memorable eyewitness accounts on social media as
humor and clickbait. They are usually mobilized by television
news networks to generate content for their programs and
social media platforms.

Cashing in on Catchphrases

In January 2016, Tulsa resident Michelle Dobyne gave an eyewitness account to local television news network *News On 6*
after her apartment complex caught fire. In the interview, a
verbal snippet from the sassy Dobyne caught the attention of
the television crew at once and they reposted the video clip on
their Facebook page: "[My neighbor] said, 'The building is on
fire!' I said, 'no what?!' I got my three kids and we bounced
out… Nuh-uh, we ain't gonna be in no fire. Not today".[141]
In a matter of hours, the clip was circulated so widely that
Dobyne went viral and became memorialized as a meme overnight. In the next few days, Dobyne's audiovisual snippet was
auto-tuned into dozens of remixes and covers, and bootleg
merchandise bearing screengrabs of her face from the news
interview and her signature catchphrase began circulating
widely on the internet. Other news networks purchased the
rights to rescreen the snippet and pursued follow-up stories
on the development of Dobyne's story, while popular, vernacular, and critical commentary on her newfound fame crowded

discursive spaces on the internet. In the weeks that followed, *News On 6* returned to the streets in search of Dobyne to provide follow-up interviews.

If this media cycle sounds familiar, it is because eyewitness virality is a tried-and-tested strategy for raking in views and traffic for news networks. Dobyne is just one of a string of eyewitness viral stars, in a trend notably kick-started by Antoine "hide yo kids" Dodson who was recounting how his sister avoided an attempted rape by a home intruder in July 2010;[142] he later launched an official Facebook page and channeled his transient fame into a music career[143] and reality show pilot.[144] Later in April 2012, Kimberly "ain't nobody got time for that" Wilkins, better known by her moniker "Sweet Brown," went viral in an interview about her building

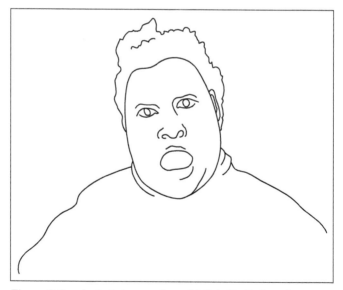

Figure 3.1.   Artist's impression of Michelle Dobyne's meme-fied facial expression. Art produced by LIBA Studio. Used with permission.

complex catching fire;[145] she then became the star of a dental care commercial[146] and made cameos in movies.[147] Other notable eyewitness viral stars include Charles "dead giveaway," Ramsey, who aided in the rescue of the Ariel Castro kidnap victims in May 2013[148] and launched an autobiography following his instant celebrity,[149] and Courtney "like a tornado girl" Barnes who gave an animated account of a car crash in June 2015.[150]

Is it Wrong to Laugh?

Eyewitness viral stars are packaged and posited, manufactured, and milked for a combination of three key ingredients that are needed to make a feel-good viral news story: Their plight that solicits a "pity factor," verbal parlance that offers a "comedic factor," and a persona of charisma curated by news networks that massages a "likeability factor." But curiously, a clear majority of "successful" eyewitness viral stars are black persons of low socioeconomic status, whose pity-comedic-likeability dimensions are premised on an intended middle-class audience's sense of distance from and exoticism toward the everyday lives of the poor and people of color. Communication scholar Catherine Knight Steel refers to similar phenomena as the "commodification of otherness" and has argued that the appropriation of marginalized cultures for memes can serve to "further marginalize rather than liberate" users in participatory culture.[151]

A handful of op-eds have used the example of Dobyne's newfound celebrity to call out traditional media for its racism and exploitation of black people. Dave Schilling of *The Guardian* called such incidents "lowbrow entertainment trenches" that "trade on stereotypes" at the expense of the "dignity" of victims,[152] while Zeba Blay of *Huffington*

Post asks whether viewers are laughing *with* Dobyne or *at* Dobyne, having denied her as "a separate, autonomous entity" and instead reading her as a stereotype of the "archetypal loud, ratchet, uneducated black woman".[153] Asha Parker of *Salon* aptly calls these formulaic routines the "memeification and auto tuning of news interviews with poor and working-class people," and denounces "society's collective urge to gawk" at them.[154]

In the wake of Michelle Dobyne's extended fame, in March 2016, I was asked by a news network to provide expert commentary on what makes eyewitness account videos go viral, what society wants to see that culminates in high viewer traffic, and why transient virality sometimes lasts longer than expected. As an anthropologist of internet culture who has been tracking viral incidents and their relationship to celebrity, I wanted to discuss the role of journalists and news networks in gatekeeping and producing eyewitness virality by celebrating stereotypes, their complicity in promulgating racism by positioning their informants as exotic, and to show how they capitalize on the misfortune of victims without funneling monetary rewards generated from viewer traffic back to their newsmakers.

The news network, however, decided to pitch a feel-good tone in their follow-up story of Dobyne, choosing instead to highlight these points: First, the reporters had not expected the clip to go viral when they decided to upload the snippet on Facebook. Second, Dobyne's reactions were authentic, albeit being widely perceived as camp and humorous. Third, Dobyne and her family have generally experienced positive outcomes because of her viral fame, even though people were selling merchandise without her permission and she was not receiving any of the profits. Lastly, they reiterated that Dobyne wished to channel her celebrity into raising awareness for domestic violence and homelessness, even though her newfound publicity did not assist in helping her out of her own dire situation, and she continues to live out of her car.[155]

In other words, to obscure the fact that they are exploiting the surplus value of Dobyne's accidental celebrity and that Dobyne's celebrity was not parlayed into social or economic progress for herself, traditional media sidestepped the racist overtones in their systemic curation and creation of eyewitness virality to assert that Dobyne was and still is very much in control of her viral fame. This denial of journalistic responsibility is hypocritical given that reporters from the news network had evidently drawn from the formulaic curation of eyewitness virality: They massaged viewers' perceptions of and approach towards Dobyne and her plight as comedic relief by reposting the Facebook clip as humor fodder; Dobyne was positioned as their "new favorite person in the entire world" for being "SO FUNNY," and that they "can't stop laughing at her interview".[156]

Who Profits?

Each time a new eyewitness viral star is plucked from obscurity and curated into instant celebrity, columnists opine that the commodity cycle of fame and commerce may give these viral stars a lifeline by allowing them to cash in on their fame, help them in their plight, and even improve their standing in life. This sentiment is so common that YouTube comments on the original and follow-up interviews (since deleted) ignore the fact that the humor of street talk may be an implicit communicative culture of black persons, or that humor in general can be mobilized as a coping strategy by those in prolonged distress. Instead, several commenters suspect that Dobyne's humor is a calculated act to generate "fifteen seconds of fame" on television. They criticize her for following a trope, for copying from Sweet Brown, and for wanting to gain fandom or celebrity.

We should be suspicious of the claim that eyewitness virality can be translated into a sustainable financial return. Once the glitz of viral clicks wears out, and the glamour of clamoring cameras and follow-up interviews dies down, and a once viral sensation is relegated into the archives of internet memory, what's there to make of the person behind the virality? Viewers seldom learn of how former viral stars are doing once media circuses have capitalized upon their instant fame for viewership, and users have expended them for internet laughs. Although a rare minority of eyewitness viral stars can groom their transient celebrity into a slightly extended but ultimately short-lived fame through endorsement deals, many of them enter this domain with little to no knowledge or preparation about how to handle their fame as a commodity. Once their initial fame dies down, some eyewitness viral stars (intentionally) return to the limelight through the mill of controversy and scandal, as in the case of Kimberly Wilkins who decided to sue Apple and several parties for the unauthorized use of her likeness and sampling of her catchphrase, a whole 12 months after she attained virality,[157] or the case of Antoine Dodson who publicly announced that he was no longer gay three years after his viral fame in 2013, despite having then used his fame to come out to the public.[158]

Eyewitness viral stars present an interesting form of internet celebrity in that at every stage of their fame cycle, several actors profit from the value of their unwitting content creation – such as news networks and print media through clickbait and follow-ups that extend public interest in the viral star, the production and hawking of bootleg merchandise whose sales do not directly benefit the viral star, and the circuit of social media content producers' covers, parodies, remixes, op-eds, and meme performances that enjoys surplus value from the viral star and their image rights without any returns or rewards to them above and beyond a namedrop or hyperlinked URL. There is little aftercare for eyewitness viral stars; their celebrity is anchored upon the milestone interview rather than any long-term investment in their public persona or personal well-being. Instead, traditional media gatekeepers reduce them into conveyable stereotypes, and they thus have limited agency to control their spiraling fame, image rights, and public perception during the cycle of virality on social media. As they are thrust into the limelight to harness viewer traffic for news networks, journalists seldom take responsibility for the instant visibility of the overnight stars they have created.

MEME PERSONALITIES

"Meme personalities" considers how ordinary people can be (unwittingly) captured in compromising circumstances or with notable expressions or gestures and become iconized as memes. Despite their image being in high circulation, the journey from meme as one-off virality to sustained and viable internet celebrity is long, arduous, and oft-times based on luck. Some of them attempt to move into the traditional media industries after attaining sufficient momentum and continued interest on social media.

A communication scholar Ryan Milner, who has studied memes critically since 2010, defines them as a "social practice"[159] of small and large conversational strands being woven into cultural tapestries through the "creation, circulation and transformation of collective texts"[160] by cultural participants. In the closing chapter of his book *The World Made Meme: Public Conversations and Participatory Media,* Milner discusses how memes can become intertwined with

the logic of capitalism and the cultural industries and ana-
lyzes how memes become reappropriated or brand-jacked to
appeal to audiences or are gatekept by the traditional media.
This section furthers Milner's observations by reviewing how
meme personalities become entangled with internet celebrity
and commerce, and introduces a life cycle of meme celebrities comprising faces of memes, meme personae, and meme
celebrities.

Faces of Memes

In the first stage, "Faces of memes," the faces of ordinary people in the images become memorialized solely for the comedic
value of the meme, through the "collective powers"[161] of users
who view, reappropriate, spread, and co-construct meaning
and value into the image. At this stage, the person and situation in the image become stereotyped as a caricature. As such,
the context of the image, the backstory of the situation, and
the original identity markers of the person photographed are
stripped away, to the point that the person becomes reduced
to a mere icon: a face of a meme. After this incubation of initial virality, and depending on public interest, users may seek
to uncover the backstory of the photograph, going beyond
the *face* in search of the actual *person* behind the meme. It is
at this point that popular media journalists often compete in
investigative work, wading through online folklore to trace
the meme's origin story, in a digital archaeology exercise that
will eventually solidify the meme's history and expose the
identity of the face photographed.

One classic example of this is "Ridiculously Photogenic
Guy" who went viral in 2012. While the origin story of this
meme has been studied in detail by meme scholars,[162] I present here a few highlights of the meme's trajectory. New York

Figure 3.2.   Artist's impression of "Ridiculously Photogenic Guy," smiling into the camera while running a marathon. Art produced by LIBA Studio. Used with permission.

resident Zeddie Watkins Little was captured on camera by photographer William King during a race in South Carolina. When the photograph was uploaded onto Flickr and then Reddit, Little's effortless smile amidst a sea of tired marathoners caught the eye of internet users. His picture became memefied and quickly attained virality. Soon, his hometown news network in Charleston traced down his father,[163] before Little himself was persuaded to be contacted by the national media on ABC's *Good Morning America*. This was his first national appearance post-meme virality, in which he candidly answered questions about his unexpected fame and indicated that he would like to retain some of his privacy by concealing the identity of his girlfriend who refused to be interviewed on camera. Shortly after, he conducted an Ask Me Anything (AMA) on Reddit, where users were curious to know about his reactions to being memed by the platform's users, what his "real life" was like, and how his meme virality had impacted his life.[164] Although he had a "meme talent manager" for a period,[165] since then Little has not taken to digital nor traditional media to extend his fame, resurface himself for other causes, or reenter the public eye. He thus remains a mere "face" of a meme. Although it is unclear why Little chose not to pursue his transient celebrity, in an interview with *Mashable*, his manager Ben Lashes revealed that "Monetising [memes] can be totally different depending [on] the thing. It's not just one formula... It's not about what you can make. It's about what you can do that's fun that people will like... You need to connect with the fanbase and make it even cooler for them".[166]

Meme Personae

In the second stage, "Meme personae," a person who has attained transient virality from being the *face* of a meme decides to extend their fame by intentionally pursuing a public persona *modeled* after the narrative for which their meme has become popular. In other words, faces of memes become meme personae when they decide to bring their iconized image to life and consistently rehash their meme narrative as an image, role, and character that they are able to monetize and profit from. This is also a practice of "further[ing] the memetic premises attached to" these initial viral images.[167]

"Bad Luck Brian" is one such example. Twenty-two-year-old Kyle Craven, a "dedicated class clown" in high school, shot to meme virality in 2012 when his friend posted his practical joke of a bad school photo to Reddit. After Craven's image became memorialized as the meme Bad Luck Brian, he underwent the same processes of being outed and backstoried by various media.[168] However, unlike Little of Ridiculously Photogenic Guy fame, Craven dedicated his new fame to a spectra of commodification practices, including merchandizing products with this meme image at Walmart and Hot Topic.[169] Craven also reenacted his new meme persona when he was flown in to guest star at internet conventions such as VidCon and Indy PopCon, appearing as Bad Luck Brian to meet with fans. Further, Craven attempted to diversify and maintain the fame of his meme persona by grooming Bad Luck Brian into internet celebrity on social media including Facebook, Twitter, Instagram, and YouTube. However, the fame of his meme was short-lived, and Craven's social media did not chalk up sufficient viewership for his meme persona to take off. He reveals that his monthly checks from YouTube revenue were "rarely more than $100," and that in the 3 years since his image went viral as Bad Luck Brian, he has only made "between $15,000 and $20,000".[170] While Bad Luck Brian still surfaces on the internet periodically, especially on meme-specific sites such as 9GAG or as reaction images on various internet forums, Craven's desire to prolong his internet celebrity did not take flight, and he has retained his day job in his family's construction business.

Where some faces of memes such as Kyle Craven intentionally groom their brief celebrity into becoming meme personae for profit with varying degrees of success, others may do so for more altruistic motivations. Sammy Griner is better

Figure 3.3.   Artist's impression of "Success Kid," eating sand with a clenched fist on the beach. Art produced by LIBA Studio. Used with permission.

known on the internet as "Success Kid," the 11-month-old baby who was photographed on the beach with a clenched fist full of sand, furrowed eyebrows, and a face of determination. The image was photographed in 2007, but first went viral in 2011 when it was remixed into an "Advice Animal" genre of memes. Unlike the trajectory of Little and Craven, Griner and his parents laid low and the child was not exposed nor publicly linked to his meme celebrity at the height of his virality, although they were paid for the use of their viral photo in some commercials in 2012.[171]

However, 4 years later in 2015, Griner and his parents came out to the press inviting users who have enjoyed his meme to contribute to a fundraising effort. The Griner family explained to *CBS News* that Success Kid's father was in urgent need of a kidney transplant, for which they were crowdfunding via the platform GoFundMe.[172] It was in this moment that the family decided to invoke Success Kid's online fame once more, revealing their backstory and public call by constructing Griner as a belated meme persona. In an interview with *The Daily Dot,* the Griner family appealed to the mobilizing power of memetic media and the historic, albeit brief, celebrity of their son: "We're the parents of 'Success Kid' for goodness sake [...] If anyone understands the power, the mass, and goodwill of the Internet, it's those of us lucky to experience it daily".[173]

Meme Celebrities

In the third stage, "Meme celebrities," a meme persona achieves extended and sustained public celebrity by growing their meme fame into a stable, sustained, and usually diversified commercial business. This requires the person behind the meme to channel their social media estates, press appearances, and commercial engagements intentionally into profit-oriented endeavors such that they become instituted as vocational public figures. Often, this specific effort involves not just the face behind the meme but also a team of public relations and publicity specialists or agencies that usually operate within the confines of traditional media structures, in a crossover that media scholars Karine Nahon and Jeff Hemsley have called "networked gatekeeping".[174]

A renowned example is that of "Grumpy Cat" – the Arizona-based cat born with dwarfism, an underbite, and a perpetual scowl – who has been a sustained meme celebrity since 2012. Grumpy Cat, whose real name is Tardar Sauce is owned by 33-year-old Tabatha Bundesen,[175] and first went viral when Bundesen's brother uploaded a photo of the pet on Reddit. Her image clocked millions of views in a matter of days, going viral on other aggregate sites such as *Buzzfeed* and even appearing on traditional news outlets such as *CNBC*, to the extent that appearance fees and image licensing rights enabled her owner Bundesen to quit her job as a waitress "within days" of Grumpy Cat's virality on social media.[176] Grumpy Cat's rampant popularity was catapulted in large part by hordes of internet users who invested creative capital and resources to remix and meme her image, allowing the cat and her owner to profit from what critical media scholar Christian Fuchs has termed the "surplus labor" of the network.[177] However, despite such extensive dispersals and the spread of her online fame, Grumpy Cat's owner also did well to consolidate her celebrity and establish origin outlets and ownership over the images. For instance, recognizing the growth potential of Grumpy Cat's new fame, owner Bundesen quickly claimed the name of the meme and established digital estates on Instagram as @realgrumpycat where she has over 2.4 million followers,[178] on Facebook as "The Official Grumpy Cat" where she has over 8 million followers,[179] and on YouTube as "Real Grumpy Cat" where she has over 37 million views.[180]

In addition to the routine circuit of press appearances, paid appearances at conventions, and image-licensing deals, owner Bundesen and meme talent manager Ben Lashes[181] have managed to convert Grumpy Cat's meme celebrity into a movie – *Grumpy Cat's Worst Christmas Ever* starring Hollywood A-listers – a book deal, a modeling career, and endorsements, sponsorships, and merchandizing deals "worth millions of dollars".[182] Grumpy Cat was named by *MSNBC* as the "Most

Influential Cat of 2012," voted the Meme of the Year at the 2013 Webby Awards,[183] and in 2017 topped the "*Forbes'* ranking of Top Pet Influencers".[184] Owner Bundesen has been known to contract highly lucrative and exclusive TV deals when granting interviews,[185] and has also begun to consult and advise "pet owners with adorable animals who might want to follow in the footsteps of" Grumpy Cat.[186]

Unwilling Memes

The three-stage model presented above illustrates how meme personalities develop into different extents of internet celebrity: faces of memes, meme personae, and meme celebrities. At each stage, the actual identity of the person behind the image attaches and sticks to the memefied image and viral celebrity differently, and these depend on the fidelity of the meme, how well the meme resonates with the audience, and other intangible idiosyncrasies such as press interest, timing, and luck. However, not all meme personalities want to be identified with their memefied image, and such unintentional and unexpected internet celebrities can be characterized as "unwilling memes."

Consider the example of the Taiwanese model Heidi Yeh, who has been unable to detach herself from her memefied image and the populist folklore surrounding her backstory since 2012. Yeh had been contracted to model for a print advertisement to promote a cosmetic surgery clinic. The image featured a family portrait comprising a glamorous and beautiful husband and wife showcasing popular cosmetic surgery outcomes in East Asia such as big eyes and noses with high bridges, accompanied by three young children whose facial features were digitally augmented to appear with eyes "exceptionally small" and "noses flat." The caption of the image read, "The only thing you'll ever have to worry about is how to explain it to the kids," implying that the parents had undergone cosmetic surgery of such good workmanship that even their children would not be able to tell the difference, and would struggle to understand why they looked starkly different from their parents.[187]

Yeh had reportedly contracted to have her image used in print media including newspaper and magazine advertisements by the clinic. However, the image made its way onto the internet when the clinic later uploaded the advertisement on its Facebook page and rival cosmetic surgery companies began to reproduce the image on their websites. In a matter of days, the

Figure 3.4.   Artist's impression of the viral meme image featuring Heidi Yeh, a husband, and three young children. Art produced by LIBA Studio. Used with permission.

image became reappropriated as a global internet meme, with a mutated backstory captioned in various translations including Arabic, English, and Japanese that the husband had sued his wife for secretly engaging in cosmetic surgery before they met, only to have her past exposed by their "ugly" children.[188] The plausibility of this narrative was bolstered in part due to the legacy of earlier tabloid coverage on a similar story, in which a husband reportedly divorced his wife and was awarded damages when his wife's plastic surgery was exposed.[189] The meme narrative bearing Yeh's image disseminated widely, shifting between print media and digital media as tabloids crafted more elaborate backstories based on hearsay, and investigative popular media journalists labored to trace down Yeh and piece together the emergence of the meme.[190]

At this point, the hoax meme had gotten so out of hand that strangers were gossiping in the presence of Yeh, her modeling opportunities reportedly decreased drastically, and her personal life suffered as a result. In addition to being cyberbullied, Yeh estimates that she lost NTD4 million in "potential earnings," and threatened to sue the clinic and advertising agency for tarnishing her image by allowing the images to circulate online.[191]

This example illustrates the stark difference between internet fame and internet infamy when memes grow in their celebrity. At this juncture, it is useful to recall that internet-native celebrities are different from celebrities who also have a presence on the internet. While the latter are bona fide public figures who have "long had to balance the benefits and detriments of media attention," the former are subject to memetic logics and pulled "from obscurity and privacy into the collective spotlight" where they are suddenly faced with a huge public audience.[192] That said, the above case studies provide evidence about how meme personalities respond to such a phenomenon with differing degrees of autonomy and good faith.

Consider the tone of the meme. Zeddie Watkins Little of "Ridiculously Photogenic Guy" and Sammie Griner of "Success Kid" were memes who were "feel good" and celebratory in tone and did not tarnish the image or reputation of either person. While Kyle Craven of "Bad Luck Brian" and Tardar Sauce of "Grumpy Cat" were portrayed in a negative light, the tone of the meme narratives was humorous and both personalities responded favorably by personifying and extending the comedic value of the meme. However, the meme narrative accusing Heidi Yeh of deceit and vanity portrayed her in a negative light, to the point of slander when users could no longer separate the meme-generated humor from the advertisement's intended wit.

Now consider the autonomy of the person behind the meme. Ridiculously Photogenic Guy and Success Kid could exercise autonomy by withholding and delaying their exposure and calculated media appearances. Bad Luck Brian and Grumpy Cat chose to wrestle back ownership over the narrative of their memes by inserting themselves into the limelight and capitalizing upon their newfound public fame. However, Heidi Yeh found herself embroiled in an extensive web of internet folklore and slander that she was unable to counter, despite her best attempts and statements to the press. Her ideo-geographical location within East Asia subjected her to double scrutiny; first internally within the region by dedicated internet users known as the "human flesh search engine" who devoted their time to tracing people's data online and exposing their deceit, and then externally among hegemonically white, Western internet users around the world who viewed this incident with ethnocentric lenses as "just another weird Asian fad." (see chapter 2 on 'exoticism').

Evidently, the trajectory and leverage of various meme personalities differ greatly especially when the tone of the meme's narrative and the autonomy of the person behind the meme are subject to manipulation. Becoming a meme personality, going viral, or attaining internet celebrity does not appeal to everyone (as in the case of Ridiculously Photogenic Guy who has retreated into oblivion) nor is it on the cards for everyone who may desire it (as in the case of Bad Luck Brian's failure to sustain his viability). For Heidi Yeh, the unwitting virality of her internet fame has changed her life far more drastically. Although an online meme dictionary has officially archived the trajectory of this meme as the "Ugly Children Lawsuit Hoax," detailing the truth behind the image and the unfolding of events,[193] her public image and reputation have not been redeemed – Yeh's pleas have not received as extensive attention as her meme narrative. Instead, the meme continues to circulate and further solidify the internet infamy from which Yeh is struggling to detach herself.

SPOTTED AND GROOMED INVESTMENTS

"Spotted and groomed investments" considers how everyday users in organically viral social media posts, especially those involving young children and teenagers, become systemically absorbed, groomed, and even exploited by the traditional media into becoming traditional celebrity icons. It involves scheduled television shows rebroadcasting the viral clip, inviting the viral stars to replicate their "act" for a live audience, disseminating these video clips on their corporate social media channels to build up their show's online viewership, and eventually contracting these personalities to star in their own recurring segments on the show. They are usually used in behind-the-scenes footage or filmed for content dedicated for broadcast on the program's social media.

In the age of social media, it is not uncommon for TV talk shows to mine the creative labor of internet users as fodder for prime-time television. Shows like *The Tonight Show*

Starring Jimmy Fallon's "Hashtag Fail" segment regularly call upon viewers to share jokes via a dedicated hashtag, while others like *Jimmy Kimmel Live!*'s "I told my kids I ate all their Halloween candy" annual video challenge invite viewers to specially stage and film pranks on young children. While both are popular examples of traditional media's solicitation of the free and willing labor of social media users to produce content for their shows, *The Ellen DeGeneres Show* is unrivalled in grooming otherwise brief brushes with fame on the internet into sustained and viable traditional celebrities.

The Ellen Factory

Some of *The Ellen DeGeneres Show*'s most groomed social media viral child stars include Kai Langer of "Bruno Mars covers" fame who went viral when aged 4 in 2013,[194] and Noah Ritter of "Apparently Kid" fame who went viral at the age of 5 in 2014.[195] They are but two in the show's brigade of viral child stars dating back to 2011, including the then 13-year-old Greyson Chance who was invited on the show after his YouTube singing and piano cover of Lady Gaga's "Paparazzi" went viral on YouTube with over 8 million views.[196] He became the first artist to be signed to Ellen DeGeneres's new record label,[197] and has at the time of writing built a career in the music industry with a studio album, two EPs, and several singles and music videos[198] with DeGeneres' or DeGeneres's support. But perhaps the most typical example of a spotted and groomed investment is that of cousins Sophia Grace Brownlee and Rosie McClelland, who began in 2011 at ages 8 and 5 as YouTube viral stars covering Nicki Minaj's "Super Bass".[199] They were subsequently groomed by *The Ellen DeGeneres Show* into a multi-platform celebrity duo known as "Sophia Grace & Rosie."

A month after their viral video, the girls were flown in from the U.K. to the U.S. in October 2011 for an interview and to reenact their viral hit.[200] In a later segment, host Ellen DeGeneres invited singer Nicki Minaj to spring a surprise on the girls where she appeared on stage as a late notice request to chat and sing with them.[201] Both videos have recorded over 32 million and 122 million views, respectively. So well received were the girls on *The Ellen DeGeneres Show* and its YouTube channel that shortly after, behind-the-scenes footage of Sophia Grace & Rosie was released on the show's You-Tube Channel,[202] in a bid to capitalize upon their virality and extend their shelf life.

Figure 3.5.   Artist's impression of Sophia Grace & Rosie performing on *The Ellen DeGeneres Show* while clad in their iconic tutu skirts and princess tiaras. Art produced by LIBA Studio. Used with permission.

Commodified Childhoods

Subsequently, the girls were subsumed into the programming of *The Ellen DeGeneres Show*, representing the show at various red-carpet events to interview traditional celebrities,[203,204,205] and starring in branded content in the YouTube content vernacular of a vlog, promoting Target,[206] Fijit,[207] and Disney,[208] among a host of clients. Sophia Grace & Rosie eventually became a bona fide staple on *The Ellen DeGeneres Show*, hosting their own segment known as "'Tea Time' with Sophia Grace & Rosie," with eight episodes between September 2012 and May 2013.[209]

The Ellen DeGeneres Show was savvy in capitalizing upon the viral uptake of Sophia Grace & Rosie early on, inserting themselves into the value chain by acting as their agents. The show's special contributions to Sophia Grace & Rosie's social media presences were acknowledged when they were flown in again to celebrate their 100 millionth view on YouTube.[210] Ellen DeGeneres eventually groomed them for their own book and movie,[211,212] and Sophia Grace exercised more ownership over her social media presence when she embarked upon Influencer commerce as a teenager.[213,214]

The Ellen DeGeneres Show's tried-and-tested formula of spotting, claiming, and grooming viral child stars on social media into celebrity investments has proven so successful that DeGeneres later co-produced a new unscripted TV show, *Little Big Shots*, hosted by veteran comedian-host Steve Harvey to showcase the talents of young children, plucked from social media posts and scouted from obscurity, and parked in the limelight of traditional media celebrity. At the time of writing, *Little Big Shots* has been renewed for a third season,[215] and an Australian edition has been successful during prime time.[216]

CROWD-PULLER CAMEOS

"Crowd-puller cameos" considers how existing internet celebrities, who already have established follower bases and viewership on social media, are invited to guest participate or even helm sections of traditional media outlets – such as print media, television, radio, and cinema – for the latter to capitalize upon their internet-native audiences and reinvigorate the former's (fading) presence and relevance in the digital age. They are usually mobilized to revitalize the falling viewership in traditional media industries. A series of case studies from Singapore evidence how this practice can be enacted on various media with varying degrees of success.

Lending Fame

Celebrated local television and film director, and recipient of the national Cultural Medallion award, Jack Neo has been shifting toward casting already-famous internet celebrities in his latest productions, several of which are the highest grossing local films annually. In various interviews with the press, he specifies that prolific internet celebrities such as "vloggers, YouTubers, [and] online personalities"[217] were cast in his movies, because they "already had some online popularity"[218] and would allow his productions to appeal to the younger market. While brief appearances have been made by the likes of popular blogger and Instagrammer Eunice Annabel Lim, who was cast in Neo's 2014 movie *The Lion Men*,[219] Neo has also personally groomed prolific YouTubers such as Tosh Zhang and Noah Yap for a series of films. The two are known for sharing controversial opinions about social issues through talking-head dialogues on YouTube.

Following this, other local producers and directors have subsequently cast various internet celebrities in cameos – such as the then top under-18 blogger Naomi Neo's cameo in director Gilbert Chan's *Ghost Child*[220] – and profited from the social media buzz among young viewers who are lured back into cinemas for local productions in the age of online streaming. Director Neo later turned to leveraging on the social capital and influence of local internet celebrities to crowdsource the casting of new blood and younger talent, by announcing that his 2015 movie, *Lingo Lingo Where You Go* will feature YouTuber Jianhao Tan.[221]

Public television channels in Singapore then followed suit by engaging popular bloggers, Instagrammers, and YouTubers in various productions.[222]

When Borrowing Backfires

The strategy of drawing upon internet celebrity cameos to lure crowds back to traditional media has also backfired due to the restrictions of traditional media censorship, the incompatibility of content between young viewers on social media and middle-aged ones on traditional media, and the difficulty in translating humor from digital subcultures to a national audience.

"MunahHirziOfficial" (MHO) made their debut in December 2008 on YouTube. They had accumulated over 142,000 subscribers and over 30 million views by April 2017 before mass deleting dozens of videos and winding up their channel.[223] MHO comprised of a Malay-Indian man and an Arab woman duo, whose internet celebrity in a country of five million racially and gender diverse peoples had been growing steadily throughout their career spanning ten year. MHO are racial/ethnic and gender/sexual minorities in Singapore and in the local Influencer industry. Their parody videos are prominent for their overt political messages albeit cloaked in drag, camp, and crass humor.

Amidst the rising popularity of social media entertainment and YouTube content production in the early to mid-2010s, ratings for traditional media outlets such as television were dipping. Producers and directors for the small and big screens, as well as editors for print media, began engaging internet celebrities to cameo in or anchor content on their respective domains in a bid to capture the youth audience. It was in this climate that Munah and Hirzi were approached by a writer from Papahan Films to star on the only Malay language national television channel, *Suria,* in their own show entitled *Munah & Hirzi: Action!,* set to premier on Wednesdays in October 2012.[224] This cross-platform strategy to lure viewership was corroborated by Munah in a press interview.[225]

Figure 3.6.   Artist's impression of MunahHirziOfficial, who are known for performing in drag. Art produced by LIBA Studio. Used with permission.

The show was to be "a drama loosely based on [their] lives as Munah & Hirzi".[226] However, amidst active advertising for the show on *Suria's* social media,[227,228] conservative Muslims expressed dissent[229], complained to the television station for selecting "inappropriate" role models,[230] and accused the duo of "anti-Islam behaviour" in the Malay print newspaper *Berita Harian*.[231] In a personal interview I conducted, Munah recounted that Facebook hate pages were set up even before the premier of their television show. The language and literacies of satire and parody that worked so well for MHO on YouTube and their social media-savvy audience did not translate well or map over properly onto television for a viewership of predominantly middle-aged, conservative Malay Muslims.

Censorship Across Platforms

Historicizing beyond the popularity of YouTube in Singapore in the early 2010s, prolific bloggers who had acquired online fame were similarly roped into traditional media projects in the mid-2000s. One such example is mrbrown who has been blogging since 1997 and is affectionately known as the "blogfather of Singapore." He was appointed as a regular columnist for the local daily tabloid *Today,* where he carried over his signature blogging humor and wit onto the newspaper. However, one column[232] was deemed too "harsh" and perceived by the Press Secretary to the Minister for Information, Communication and the Arts (MICA) to be a "satirical attack on the government".[233]

The column had discussed a string of social issues pertaining to income and class inequality in the country, and mrbrown was accused in the Press Secretary's public letter in the same newspaper of "distorting the truth" and having "calculated to encourage cynicism and despondency".[234] Within the same week, mrbrown's column was suspended and he was fired from the newspaper,[235] inciting a small and dispersed public demonstration of 30 people outside City Hall.[236] Where freedom of expression and interpretations of satire may be more flexible and accommodating within the context of the internet, the tone and discourse does not always translate well into traditional media platforms. Evidently, harnessing the attention value and influence of internet celebrities as crowd-puller cameos for ailing traditional media industries can be a risky investment.

WEAPONIZED MICROCELEBRITY

"Weaponized microcelebrity" considers how highly prolific microcelebrities, whose content has the potential to polarize public opinion, are hijacked for attention – or "attention hacked" – by traditional media through disproportionate and sensationalist coverage, such that their viral persona, fame, and content become reappropriated as placeholders for various causes. This usually begins with an instigator "calling out" a microcelebrity over an issue, swiftly escalates to numerous follow-up stories that often distort the original incident from second-hand reportage, and results in waves of new coverage from various angles to extend readers' interest in the issue. They are often mobilized by the companion digital estates of traditional media networks and various digital media platforms. A prolific incident that exemplifies such a sequence of attention hacking is *The Wall Street Journal's* accusations of anti-Semitism against Swedish YouTuber "PewDiePie."

Context and Control

On February 14, 2017, *The Wall Street Journal* published a paywalled article and accompanying video accusing

27-year-old Felix Kjellberg, better known by his moniker PewDiePie, of publishing "anti-Semitic posts," and
announced that Disney had ended their partnership with
him.[237] Accordingly, the paper took offense to PewDiePie's
content and informed Disney of the infraction, which result-
ed in the company – whose Maker Studios network partners with PewDiePie – terminating their contract with the
YouTuber. Among a checklist of infringements – including a
black-humored prank on "Funny Guys" from the cash-for-
jobs site Fiverr, who were paid to hold up a sign that read,
"Death To All Jews" – the paper argued that PewDiePie had
performed the Nazi salute and donned a Nazi uniform in
his videos.

In a media ecology saturated with Influencers, wan-
nabes, and traditional media attempting to shift into digital
spaces, this news was significant as PewDiePie was among
the most-watched, renowned, and viable icons in the digital
Influencer industry. He was the most subscribed and highest paid YouTuber in 2016.[238] Following the dissolution of
partnership by Disney, platform partner YouTube Red also
dropped PewDiePie from its stable, terminated his upcoming series, and removed him from its advertising program.[239]
After the longtail amplification of the incident by hundreds of
media outlets and fellow YouTubers, PewDiePie removed the
offensive video and addressed the public (instead of his usual
subculture of followers) in a response video.

In it PewDiePie lamented that the media has thus far only
focused on his earnings and wealth, ignoring other aspects
such as his charity work. He argued that traditional media
fear the influence of YouTubers, and so participate in clickbait and slip to tabloid standards in their coverage of social
media stars, to discredit them and undermine their economic
value. Most crucially, PewDiePie asserted that *The Wall Street
Journal* took his jokes out of context by misrepresenting

them as intentional hate posts and he went on to situate the accused jokes in the context of their original videos. He admitted that he is unable to control the fact that hate groups misappropriate his joke videos as hate content but denounced them in a public statement. Finally, PewDiePie apologized for taking his jokes too far, said he was learning from the lesson, and acknowledged that there are consequences for his actions. Thanking fellow YouTubers for coming out in support of him, he ended the video.

YouTubers Talk Back

Some of the fellow YouTubers who published their own commentaries to call out the character assassination of PewDiePie by traditional media, as well as the impasse caused by his black humor, include the most prolific and profitable users such as "Markiplier"[240], "h3h3Productions"[241], and Philip DeFranco.[242] Collectively, these and other YouTubers volunteered cross-referential and cultural translation work, juxtaposing the press-quoted snippets of PewDiePie's videos against the context of the originals. Several illustrations were foregrounded to situate the newly viral snippets in the entirety of their original videos, supported with context, as informed by the community norms of humor among YouTubers.

For instance, while *The Wall Street Journal* circulated a still image of PewDiePie supposedly making the Nazi salute, this was merely him extending his arm and pointing offscreen. But the paper had conveniently renarrativized this gesture since PewDiePie's hand and pointed fingers were not visible in the still and could be de- and re-contextualized. Additionally, the paper had lifted a clip of PewDiePie donning a uniform and watching Hitler videos and accused him of being a Nazi sympathizer, when this was actually the second half of a longer snippet in which PewDiePie first refuted earlier media accusations that he was a Nazi supporter, and then jokingly donned a British military uniform while pretending to watch clips of Hitler's speech to depict how he feels the media views him. With this added contextual topography, several YouTubers expressed outrage over *The Wall Street Journal*'s intentional negation of the cultural context and vernacular implicit within the communicative norms of YouTube subcultures.

Moreover, the YouTubers collectively argued that traditional media like *The Wall Street Journal* are attacking YouTubers and Influencers in a "huge smear campaign",[243] meant to capitalize upon the digitally native popularity of PewDiePie to reel in clicks for their own clickbaity "juicy headlines".[244] Although many YouTubers also admitted that they are constitutive of the self-referential, discursively networked, clickbaity culture of YouTube, in which the genre of "response" videos takes advantage of trending topics to gather views, they also felt a genuine need to emphasize that the paper's intention and incentive was primarily monetarily inspired rather than concerned with advancing social justice, serving as a chilling effect to rein in other YouTubers and reassert traditional media's growing presence in digital spaces.

As Influencers such as PewDiePie become iconized as enemies/heroes of the (alternative) media, they also become placeholders against whom people can align themselves to exemplify larger moral values and political allegiances. Even though YouTube celebrities have largely framed the scandal as an attack by traditional media that are vying for a share of the attention economy in digital spaces, by islands of politicized spectators, PewDiePie has been lionized as a symbol of the struggle for free speech, as a proponent against fake news, and another chess piece in the spillover effects of vulnerable global media ecologies.

CONCLUSION

In this chapter, we reviewed five distinct types of internet celebrities and examined how they have different symbiotic and parasitic relationships with traditional media.

Eyewitness viral stars are usually generated and exploited by television news networks for viral views, in which case their value flows from traditional media to internet celebrity, but ultimately feeds back to sustain traditional media traffic; meme personalities profit from their fame to different extents by intentionally engaging with traditional media industries, and thus see value arising in internet celebrity, taking pit stops in traditional media to gain wider traction, before returning to a more amplified and stable form of internet celebrity; spotted and groomed investments are viral social media acts plucked from the internet and groomed in the traditional television industry for internet-friendly content, hence their value originates in internet celebrity, gets quickly absorbed by traditional media, and then flows in a circuit between traditional media and internet celebrity by mutually amping up each outlet's traffic; crowd-puller cameos lend their social media fame

Table 3.1.   Value flows between internet celebrity and traditional media for each type of internet celebrity.

Internet celebrity type	Value flows between internet celebrity (IC) and traditional media (TM)
Eyewitness viral stars	$TM \rightarrow IC \rightarrow TM$
Meme personalities	$IC \rightarrow TM \rightarrow IC'$
Spotted and groomed investments	$IC \rightarrow TM \longleftrightarrow IC'$
Crowd-puller cameos	$IC \rightarrow TM$
Weaponized microcelebrity	$IC \longleftrightarrow TM$

to traditional media productions and revitalize and lure over their young viewership, which presents a straightforward value flow from internet celebrity toward traditional media; and weaponized microcelebrity personalities are attention hacked by various traditional and digital media outlets when their infractions become fair game for public commentary and placeholders for a longtail of social issues, resulting in a cyclic loop between internet celebrity and traditional media where value flows back and forth in cycles. In the next chapter, we will focus on a specific form of vocational internet celebrity known as "Influencers" and learn about key developments in that industry.

4

FROM INTERNET CELEBRITIES
TO INFLUENCERS

As the phenomenon of internet celebrity has been adopted and adapted throughout various structures and institutions in society, its practice and culture are no longer confined to popular culture, entertainment, or mere frivolity. In fact, the wide uptake and global prominence of internet celebrity have cultivated an elite economic group that has been able to turn their digital fame into a self-brand and eventually a business. In this chapter, I focus on the genre of internet celebrity known as Influencers, who are vocational, sustained, and highly branded social media stars. They are a critical form of internet celebrity given their ability to attract and maintain a sizable following on their social media platforms, through highly engaging and personalized content production, which can be used as conduits of information to amplify messages. Here, I briefly discuss the architecture of the Influencer industry including front-end and back-end endeavors, the emerging shadow economy that supports the black market of Influencer commerce, the global implications of Influencer culture pertaining to economics, legality, culture, and social issues, and finally a few recent shifts in the ways in which Influencers are practicing and managing their fame on the internet.

Before we begin, here is a brief note on my capitalization of "Influencer": The term "influencer" has been used in business studies to describe a model of marketing and advertising that targets key individuals who exert influence over a large pool of potential customers. These key individuals generally filter and disseminate content for their audience and include industry retailers and manufacturers, journalists and magazine editors, and more recently, high-profile social media users. Business scholars have studied such influencers in terms of where they are located within communication flows,[245] how they are used by brands,[246,247] some of their marketing strategies,[248,249] and their impact on business models.[250] However, as an anthropologist focused on the culture and role of Influencers in society, I distinguish the "influencer" as a mediator situated in business research from the "Influencer" that I investigate as a vocation and practice focused on social media-based, multimedia, fame on the internet.

ARCHITECTURE OF THE INFLUENCER INDUSTRY

As iterated in Chapter 1, the structural and cultural histories of internet celebrity may differ and exude nuance depending on the sociocultural climate and ideo-geographies of a region. As such, to lay out the architecture of the Influencer industry briefly, in this section I draw on my research on Influencers in Singapore since the late 2000s to demonstrate some of the key arms and formal organization in the industry.

Blogshops, Commercial Blogging, and Influencers

Although the term Influencer only came in vogue in the mid-2010s, the practice of Influencer culture has a longer history. In Singapore, the emergence of Influencers was rooted in the "blogshop" industry from the mid-2000s, where young women were self-modeling and selling used clothing on blog platforms such as OpenDiary, LiveJournal, Blogspot, and Xanga, literally repurposing blogs into online shops. Several blogshop owner-models began "side blogs" where they would narrate their personal lives in a diary-style format, while also posting pictures of themselves in clothes they were trying to hawk on the internet.[251]

As this local economy grew and prominent blogshop models, owners, and owner-models accumulated extensive fame and a loyal following, the more established blogshops began importing new clothing from regional fashion manufacturers such as Bangkok, Shenzhen, and Guangzhou for their growing clientele. Eventually, the most successful of these blogshops branched off into full-fledged online fashion stores,

Figure 4.1. Artist's impression of the front page of a typical blogshop, featuring young women modeling various clothes. Art produced by LIBA Studio. Used with permission.

manufacturing their own labels and exclusive designs, while maintaining their disclosive personal diary narratives on blogs and new social media platforms.[252] By the mid-2010s, several of these blogshops-turned-fashion retailers expanded into brick-and-mortar shops by first renting racks at aggregate fashion stores, running pop-up shops, renting large warehouses to double up as office spaces and fashion stores, and later leasing dedicated storefronts for their fashion lines.

Throughout this steady growth of the blogshop industry, many readers of blogs and customers of these stores saw the value of using personal narration to capture an audience. A stream of young women thus began blogging about their everyday lives as lived in the genre of "lifestyle" blogging, to foster intimacies with their customers and build a personal brand to market their blogshops. Initially, only a handful of blogshops ran personal blogs to engage with customers. But, as the blogshop industry boomed, more blogshop owners and models specifically curated commercial blogs to hone their personal brands. Such commercial blogs commanded such steady, high traffic that these lifestyle bloggers were attracting and soliciting paid ad spaces, receiving freebies in exchange for shout-outs and mentions, engaged for endorsements and sponsorships, and even appointed dedicated spokespersons at the physical roadshows of various brands. It is at this juncture that they formally became "commercial bloggers".[253] As social media apps grew popular in Southeast and East Asia, many of these women naturally expanded their digital estates to form the first cohort of Influencers in Singapore.

Influencer Agencies and Managers

With the Influencer industry in Singapore expanding rapidly, some Influencers became signed to management agencies while others remained freelancers. Those who were contracted to agencies were usually either the most successful Influencers who were very much sought after by clients, budding Influencers who were exhibiting growth potential and being groomed by managers, or aspirational users who were keen to formally engage in Influencer commerce through in-house training. In exchange for management services, such as the negotiation of fair work conditions and quality checks on sponsored social media content, a percentage of the revenue earned by contracted Influencers is apportioned as commission.[254]

Two of the earliest Influencer management agencies to launch were Nuffnang and Gushcloud, in 2007[255] and 2011,[256] respectively. They managed Influencers and functioned as an intermediary between Influencers and clients. Later, some smaller companies, such as blog platform My Fat Pocket and agency The Influencer Network also began to manage contracted Influencers who were signed exclusively to their firms, as well as freelance Influencers. Influencer managements aggregate Influencers across genres and pitch them to clients seeking Internet personae for endorsements, sponsorships, and social media marketing campaigns.

However, this is not to say that all uncontracted Influencers were at the bottom of the barrel, as several highly successful Influencers were able to sustain their businesses and act as independent agents for themselves. Later, several Influencers established their own agencies to broker contracts for themselves and for the newer Influencers who they were grooming within their company, often with the help of employed staff. As such, unsigned Influencers generally belong to one of three categories:

The first category comprises Influencers who can operate independently to attract and negotiate with clients because they are exceedingly popular and command strong bargaining power. As independent Influencers, they do not have to pay a broker's commission and can increase their overall revenue, although this may mean a less regular stream of work.

The second category is made up of Influencers whose daytime jobs do not allow them to be under other contractual agreements. These are usually women in civil service jobs who are unable to receive monetary payment for their advertising services, and so attend exclusive events and receive products for free, in exchange for producing reviews on social media.

The third category consists of new and upcoming Influencers, or those who have not yet garnered a sustainable following despite being in the industry for some time. These Influencers do not yet command the attention of a sizable following on the web and are not as sought after as other Influencers. They will have to market themselves and rely on personal networks to be noticed by Influencer managers. In general, most Influencers, especially in the lifestyle genre, aim to be signed to an Influencer management, as it is a mark of prestige; as well, the Influencer management oversees their career trajectories, brings them more publicity via corporate-wide campaigns, and increases their pool of available work.

Generating Income

In general, Influencers earn revenue in three main ways. A primary mode of revenue is from advertorials, which is a highly personalized, narrative advertising format that resembles an opinion-editorial.[257] The more popularly advertised products and services are facial and beauty products and services, plastic surgery and cosmetic enhancements, apparel and fashion, food and beverages, and travel. As of the mid-2010s, Influencers could earn up to SGD100,000 per sponsorship although most "A-list" bloggers are able to earn at least SGD10,000 in profits monthly from their Influencer advertising business alone. Most Influencers can average a monthly income of SGD2,000 to 5,000.

The second mode is to sell advertising space on their blogs and social media platforms. Influencers are contacted by clients to post banners that link to their website in a bid to capture a share of these Influencers' immense followings. Each Influencer usually has her own rate and "package deal." For instance, one Influencer tells me a 300-pixel x 450-pixel space on her blog costs SGD320 per three-day slot, while another sells a 0.5 cm x 0.5 cm button for SGD200 per year. However,

Figure 4.2.   Artist's impression of the landing page of a typical Influencer's blog, featuring static banner ads in the header and side bars. Art produced by LIBA Studio. Used with permission.

Influencers who are contracted to management agencies may have their advertising rates regulated by their managers.

A third mode of income is from selling wares. Influencers who have garnered overwhelming popularity have been known to hawk used personal items on their blogs and on Instagram. These "pre-loved" – a euphemism for second-hand – apparel, accessories, and knick-knacks are well received by followers, some of whom have expressed a desire to own "a piece of" the Influencers through their second-hand possessions. Occasionally, followers have even resorted to bidding to secure an item. Moreover, the most adored and business-savvy of these Influencers usually go on to launch their own brands in the areas of beauty, fashion, and food and beverages, using their Influencer fame to propel their business ventures.

SHADOW ECONOMIES OF THE INFLUENCER INDUSTRY

As far back as 2010, controversies and under-table exchanges had already arisen in the Influencer industry, such as whether Influencers should pay for the products and services they sample to produce reviews.[258,259] In recent years, some Influencers have been known to request for freebies outright, in exchange for guaranteed positive reviews and free advertising on their social media. In response to this, service providers have begun to ban Influencers from using their premises or from soliciting complimentary services.[260] While these controversies may be deemed borderline unethical, others are more systemic exploitations of social media, algorithms, and the industry's cultural norms to boost one's portfolio. In this section, we discuss three such shadow economies – bots, spam, and self-amplification groups – and reactions from social media platforms to these vernacular attention-garnering strategies.

Bot Followers & Account Purges

The market value of Instagram Influencers is usually proportionate to the number of followers they have. Many clients who engage Instagram Influencers for advertorials and brand ambassadorships pay them according to their "reach," or the number of potential consumers who would come across Influencers' content. To boost their follower count artificially, and thus their market values, some Influencers have taken to purchasing "fake followers" from third-party accounts that use bots to create hundreds of dummy accounts to follow other accounts, or function as "clickfarms" to "like" an Influencer's post mechanically in order to inflate numbers artificially. The market rate of such fake followers is reportedly between $7 and $14 for 500 followers.[261,262]

While some Influencers purposefully purchase bot followers, others are subject to sabotage when "fake" followers and likes are purchased for them in bulk, resulting in an artificial boost in follower counts overnight. Since these incidents are difficult to trace, they usually become known when Influencers post updates about a sudden and dubious increase of thousands or tens of thousands of followers to their account overnight. As part of their damage control, Influencers would forewarn potential clients of this sabotage, temporarily set their accounts to private, and quickly screen through their lists of latest followers to block bots and recalibrate their follower counts.

In December 2014, Instagram responded to the proliferation of artificial inflation by initiating the first of several attempts to delete bots, fake accounts, and inactive accounts from their database systemically.[263] This was dubbed "the Instagram Purge," "the Instagram Rapture," and "the Instagram Clean-up" by users and popular press outlets alike. As a result, prolific Instagram users with high follower counts, such as traditional media celebrities and Influencers, experienced huge losses. Influencers who were affected by the Purge reacted in two main ways: those who had lost a sizable proportion of their followers immediately set their accounts to private amidst condemnation and critique from fellow Influencers and followers; others who had emerged relatively unscathed capitalized on the exposé to reassert their authenticity through narratives of disclosure. They began to announce their "drop count" voluntarily on various social media in a bid to display a sense of honesty and integrity, and to subtly reaffirm that their "slight drop" in numbers was merely attributed to inactive accounts rather than bought followers.

To encourage followers to empathize, Influencers asked followers to report on their own "loss" as an act of commiseration, to reiterate that "small losses" are normal, and to diffuse attention from Influencers' own "drop counts." By gloating over rivals' losses, redeeming themselves from previous accusations, and disclosing taboo contemplations, these Influencers manage to manipulate the Purge to perform wearing guises of authenticity for their followers.

Hashtag Spam & Shadow Ban

Another way in which users have been gaming algorithms on Instagram is through hashtag spam. At the time of writing, Instagram allows up to 30 hashtags per caption. Several online service providers are dedicated to aggregating in real time the best 30 hashtags pertaining to specific functions (i.e., getting likes, garnering "comments", or soliciting "follows") or themes (i.e., animals, fashion, nature) that Instagram followers may use. They include the website TagBlender[264] and mobile app Hashtags For Likes[265], which constantly update the hashtags with the highest traffic that users can copy and paste into their captions to generate more traffic. Although many Influencers (and aspirants) utilize this tactic to expand their audience reach, such vernacular practices spam and negate the interest communities that have organically formed around Instagram hashtags when used sincerely.

In response, in early 2017, Instagram began removing posts with hashtag spam from its public feed such that they cannot be discovered "by chance" by users, in a move dubbed the "shadow ban" by users and media commentators.[266] In its public statement, Instagram asserted that businesses who use their platform should not rely primarily on hashtags for publicity but have clear business objectives.[267] They recommend branding strategies such as cultivating a distinct visual presence, telling good stories, and being creative.

Instagram Pods & Twitter Decks

Given the onslaught of bots and fake followers, hashtag spam and the vernacular gaming of platforms, social media like Instagram and Twitter began modifying their algorithms to change the way users experience content. For instance, both platforms no longer show posts in chronological order by default,[268,269] resulting in brands and Influencers having to amplify the reach of their content by ensuring that it registers the most engagement through likes in the first few minutes of being posted. Although strategies for opting out of these new algorithmic patterns have been circulating on popular news media,[270,271] it is unlikely that opting out is the norm for a clear majority of users who usually accommodate these gradual changes on social media.

To combat these new algorithmic changes while ensuring that they do not give in to industry taboos such as purchasing fake followers and likes, some Influencers have formed informal networks to amplify each others' content within secret circuits known as "Instagram pods"[272] and "Twitter decks"[273]. In both circuits, small groups of 10 to 20 Influencers pool their follower networks and potential exposure by mutually amplifying each others' content, either through narratively promoting others in their clan or by systematically liking, retweeting, or commenting on posts by Influencers in their clan, such that their own followers may also see them. Although Influencer pods and decks are not technically in violation of any platform guidelines, ethically they disrupt the supposedly sacred rule of organically attaining viewer traffic for Influencer content. It is also difficult for such groups to be traced or exposed, given that it requires a keen eye across several Influencers' digital estates and active corroboration of content, time stamps, and networks to ascertain that a pod or deck is truly at work. Not surprisingly, some hawk-eyed social media users have already begun to expose such Influencer groups, calling upon others to boycott them.[274]

GLOBAL IMPLICATIONS OF THE INFLUENCER INDUSTRY

The Influencer industry has progressed and advanced across several industry verticals and areas of society. Yet, news reports seem to be stuck in a backdated time loop as they continually express surprise at the fact that Influencers can command a sizable earning[275] and that brands want to work with them,[276] while asserting that the workings of the Influencer industry is still mysterious[277] and a secret weapon.[278] Polarizing coverage also constantly reiterates that the industry is simultaneously on the rise[279] and on the decline.[280] To keep abreast of the global implications of the Influencer industry thus far, this section surveys international news reports on Influencers in 2017, and summarizes some of the controversial blows and innovative debuts that have taken place in the industry in relation to economics, legality, culture, and social issues.

Economics

On the plane of economics, developments have taken place in relation to corporate Influencer schemes and educational Influencer programs, the structures of Influencer agencies, and Influencer enterprises.

American online retail company Amazon launched the Amazon Influencer Program in which selected Influencers in their stable are now able to earn commissions on products sold through their recommendations;[281] Chinese short-form video social network Musical.ly, which is popular among young users who lip-sync on the app, dedicated a $50 million Creator Fund to groom some of their most prolific users into becoming media Influencers;[282] Chinese Influencer incubators have successfully groomed Influencers for the e-commerce industry, resulting in talents earning up to $46 million annually;[283] and Chinese universities have begun to offer classes and degrees tailor-made for Influencer-aspirants, including courses on makeup, modeling, fashion, aesthetics, and public relations.[284]

Singaporean Influencer agency Gushcloud was acquired by South Korean media conglomerate Yello Digital Marketing to develop Influencer commerce further in the Southeast and East Asia regions, including partnerships with traditional entertainment industries such as a $3 million investment from the K-pop record label YG Entertainment;[285] American content marketing company Ginzamarkets, Inc. bought out Tokyo-based Influencer marketing platform

Withfluence in order to expand their content promotion on a more global scale;[286] American public relations company Citizen Relations established a new arm of Influencer marketing by purchasing The Narrative Group, a contemporary lifestyle agency focusing on Influencer commerce;[287] and search engine Google and social media app Snapchat acquired Influencer marketing firms FameBit and Flite for $36 million and $42 million, respectively, to serve their advertisers' needs to connect with social media-based audiences better.[288]

Vietnamese-American beauty YouTuber Michelle Phan relaunched her beauty subscription brand ipsy after taking a gap year for mental health issues;[289] black American Peaches Monroee, who coined the catchphrase "eyebrows on fleek," admitted that she has not received any compensation from the major corporations and celebrity Influencers who have profited from her cultural work, and decided to crowdfund her new beauty line;[290] Italian fashion blogger Chiara Ferragni, better known by her moniker "The Blonde Salad," parlayed her own fashion brand into an upmarket boutique in Milan;[291] and Macau-born Influencer Yoyo Cao became one of dozens of Asian Influencers to launch their own fashion labels at international fashion weeks.[292]

Legality

On the plane of legality, developments have taken place regarding advertising disclosures, dishonest marketing, astroturfing, taxes, contentious content, and abuse on social media.

New national advertising regulations have been announced in places such as Australia,[293] the U.K.,[294] and the U.S.,[295] requiring Influencers to indicate the status of sponsorship and paid content on their social media posts clearly; American organizers of the Fyre Festival, which capitalized on the visibility labor of Influencers, were sued for dishonest marketing;[296] some Influencers (and Influencer-aspirants) were exposed for going on the black market to purchase "verified" statuses for their Instagram accounts;[297] around the world Influencers were exposed for purchasing fake followers to boost their profile statistics;[298] and a shadow economy of scam companies have been constructing fake Influencer profiles using stolen or stock images to net sponsors and endorsements.[299]

Street style photographers at Milan Fashion Week demanded that Influencers stop using their images to advertise sponsored brands on social media, without adequately remunerating photographers;[300] Tomi Lahren, the anchor from American talk show *The Blaze* lost access to her prominent Facebook account after being fired from the company;[301] Singaporean teenage YouTuber Amos Yee appealed for political asylum in the U.S. after being arrested for political persecution due to his controversial vlogs;[302] and the American family Influencers behind the "DaddyOFive" channel were arrested on allegations of committing child abuse in their YouTube videos.[303]

Culture

On the plane of culture, developments have emerged around racism, politics and religiosity, and notions of authenticity.

Swedish YouTuber PewDiePie's satire and black humor have seen him being accused of Nazism and racism (see Chapter 3); Filipina-Australian Influencer "lilymaymac" was called out for old tweets in which she expressed feelings of "#white fever" and prejudices against Asian men;[304] Singaporean YouTube channel "RyanSylvia," run by the Night Owl Cinematics production company has experienced internet hate for casual racism in their videos;[305] white American League of Legends Twitch streamer "Pink_Sparkles" was cyberbullied and received racist threats after revealing that she was newly dating an Asian man;[306] and Swiss beauty blogger Chanel Brusco was called out for casual racist slurs against East Asians in her review of Korean beauty products.[307]

Ten-year-old Canadian vlogger Dylan, known as "Sceneable" on YouTube, went viral for preaching communism;[308] Cambodian monks are going viral and amassing microcelebrity for livestreaming;[309] and Mormon mommy blogger "Wife with a Purpose" was called out for spreading alt-right hate in her content.[310]

Black American rapper Bow Wow was called out for faking an Instagram post resulting in the "Bow Wow Challenge" meme, in part made viral by Influencers;[311] Australian wellness blogger Belle Gibson was fined $410,000 after being sued for faking cancer and misleading followers that she had self-cured;[312] and young children on YouTube are leaving fake comments on popular videos that their parents or pets have died to solicit sympathy through likes.[313]

Social Issues

Finally, on the plane of social issues, developments have progressed regarding sexualization and exploitation, the commercialism of young children in the media, vulnerability and hardship, and the spillover effects of the Influencer industry into other economies in society.

Thirteen-year-old American Danielle Bregoli of viral catchphrase "Cash Me Ousside" fame has continued to be hypersexualized by the media and by followers;[314] young women continue to be recruited and groomed for the highly profitable sexcam industry in countries like Romania;[315] and

Singaporean students who uploaded dressing room selfies to the likes of Instagram fashion Influencers became the target of a Tumblr blog that sexualized their images.[316]

Two-and-half-year-old Chinese toddler "Xiaoman" became a commercial internet sensation following her parents' daily uploads of her mealtimes;[317] 6-year-old Ryan of "Ryan ToysReview" became one of the highest earning YouTube Influencers by earning $11 million in 2017;[318] and 6-year-old Japanese child "Coco" has been groomed into a fashion Influencer by her parents who own a vintage store.[319]

Taiwanese-American "KevJumba," who was a pioneer vlogger on YouTube, returned to vlogging after a long hiatus and life-threatening accident;[320] and couple Influencers around the world, such as Colleen Ballinger and Joshua David Evans, are publicly vlogging their breakups to decouple their narrative and rebrand themselves as individuals.[321]

A group of Asian-American YouTubers, led by Japanese-American vlogger Ryan Higa, produced a satirical K-pop song that ended up ranking in legitimate music charts in the entertainment industry;[322] food flat lays and café shots made popular by Instagram Influencers have pushed restaurants to renovate their interiors entirely to attract young diner-Instagrammers;[323] and the Museum of Ice Cream was set up in San Francisco specifically to provide Instagrammable-backdrops for clients and visitors to produce Influencer-quality images.[324]

Taken together, the economic, legal, cultural, and social impact of the Influencer industry has stimulated innovative forms of digital labor on the internet, encouraged an increasing uptake of young people in entrepreneurship, generated new models of work life, fostered cross-cultural literacies, raised the value of digital estates, demonstrated the potential of networked social movements, and seen the spread of vernacular practices on a global scale.

RECENT SHIFTS IN THE INFLUENCER INDUSTRY

As iterated earlier, the origins of the Influencer industry can be traced back to various cultural and platformed histories, such as blogshop modeling and selling on blog platforms in Singapore, or bedroom webcamming via webcams in the U.S. As more digital tools and social media become available to users, Influencers migrate in and out of various platforms in waves. To sustain users' interest and respond to vernacular innovations of their functions, social media platforms continually update their interfaces corresponding to functions that are most popularly used in the market.

In one such instance, August 2016 saw Instagram introducing "Stories," which allows users to upload multiple images and videos in a slideshow format with a 24-hour lifespan.[325] It is likely that part of this move was motivated by a substantial proportion of Influencers who were cross-platforming between Instagram and Snapchat, using the former to maintain their pristine but static photography feeds while uploading transient 24-hour video diaries in a more casual format on Snapchat.[326] In several media interviews, Instagram even admitted that their new function was a copy of Snapchat's Stories,[327] and in their press release alluded to their knowledge that the dominant users on each platform have cultivated distinct cultural norms of approved behavior:

> *With Instagram Stories, you don't have to worry about overposting. Instead, you can share as much as you want throughout the day — with as much creativity as you want. [...] Instagram has always been a place to share the moments you want to remember. Now you can share your highlights and everything in between, too.*

This move by Instagram clearly signaled two things: first, that the curation rhetoric of Instagram as a regulated repository with optimum posting times and frequencies to maximize viewer perception is being acknowledged, but also that Instagram wants users to break out of this normative practice popularized by its top Influencer Instagrammers so that more content will be shared more frequently; and second, that the curation rhetoric of Instagram as a highlight reel for only one's "best images" is being acknowledged, and also that Instagram wants users to content dump on its platform instead of cross-platforming (over to Snapchat, for instance) to post their content.

Extrapolating from this nod to the extensive impact and mobilizing power of Influencer practices, in this section I review five recent shifts in the Influencer industry, briefly outlining how the cultural norms of these prolific and elite social media users are quietly innovating.

Archive Culture → Streaming Culture

Considering the onslaught of live-streaming functions on social media such as Snapchat and Instagram, and dedicated live-streaming platforms, such as Twitch and Periscope that are popular in the Anglo-North and Bigo and BeLive that are popular in East Asia, Influencers are shifting from a culture of archived semi-permanent content to one of streaming always-transient content. More specifically, the aesthetic of Influencer content is expanding from the feels of pristine, high-quality images that were dominantly "repository format" social media, to include simultaneously haphazard, spontaneous, raw footage on "transient format" social media.

This is largely motivated by followers' cultivations of perpetual "FOMO," or the "fear of missing out." The attention

Figure 4.3.   Artist's impression of a live-streaming session in progress, featuring live comments and an assortment of emoji and tokens of appreciation streaming in from viewers. Art produced by LIBA Studio. Used with permission.

economy of Influencer content is a system in which content is in abundance, but consumers' attention spans are limited. In other words, attention becomes a scarce resource which has to be competed for in a "war of eyeballs".[328] While repository social media is more permanent and allows followers to return to the material at their own pace and in their own time, transient social media is ephemeral and demands that followers assign it full attention in the narrow window during which it is available for viewing.

Tasteful Consumption → Amateur Aesthetic

In the wake of conscientiously maintained luxury feeds, the accessibility once promised by the rise of Influencers is being eroded as their practice and personae appear more unattainable due to barriers of entry such as cost, social capital, or cultural capital. The live, moving-image affordances of streaming apps tend to enable for little modification and "photoshopping," and the basic editing affordance of apps like Snapchat restrict modification to preset filters, stickers, and scribbles. The Influencer ecology is thus moving from its peak of tasteful consumption formats toward an amateur aesthetic that feels less staged and thus more authentic.

In fact, in the age of picture-perfect, luxury-oriented, hyper-feminine Instagram Influencers, who have dominated the Instagram economy thus far, authenticity has become less of a static quality and more of a performative ecology and parasocial strategy with its own bona fide genre and self-presentation elements. I have studied the rise of such performative authenticity as "calibrated amateurism," or a

> practice and aesthetic in which actors in an attention economy labor specifically over crafting contrived authenticity that portrays the raw aesthetic of an amateur, whether or not they really are amateurs by status or practice, by relying on the performance ecology of appropriate platforms, affordances, tools, cultural vernacular, and social capital.[329]

The aesthetic of calibrated amateurism has a leveling effect because Influencers appear less constructed, less filtered, more spontaneous, and more real, thus fostering feelings of relatability and authenticity.

Influencers' transits toward the amateur aesthetic have also been acknowledged and adapted by Instagram, which in July 2017 began encouraging users to create multiple accounts with the following prompt:[330] "Share a Different Side of Yourself. Create a private account to share photos and videos with a close group of followers."

By newly encouraging multiple accounts through their new affordances and direction prompts, Instagram is bringing into officialdom the practice of "Finstagramming." "Finstagrams" (fake Instagrams, as opposed to "Rinstagrams" or real Instagrams) have long proliferated among young users. Multiple accounts encourage followers and viewers to engage in cross-platform hopping, watching, and matching. They imply that we all have back stages and hidden secrets on display on parallel platforms, if only our audience knows where to look and how to look for these Easter eggs. Thus, emerges a new game in the attention economy where the pursuit is no longer some semblance of authentic disclosure, but a competitive investigation into and comparison of the different strands of selfhood that a single user may put out on multiple platforms through multiple usernames promoting multiple personae.

Platformed Fame → Cross-Platform Influence

Although Influencers usually dominate on one or two platforms with others being complementary digital estates, they still regularly maintain several profiles at once and may use each medium for specific content and purposes. Advertisers have also contributed to the rise of such multitasking, where it is common for Influencer agencies to pitch Influencers to clients in the form of "packages," such that a single campaign assigned to an Influencer may be marketed rather distinctly across various platforms to cross-traffic and circulated to a wider audience. For instance, an Influencer who is attending a fashion event may post pre-event dressing room updates on Snapchat Stories, post videos of the event on Instagram Stories, post formal images from the event as advertorials in an Instagram photo, push out tweets throughout the day to engage with followers on Twitter, and finally upload a long-form vlog of the entire event later on YouTube. Influencer commerce is thus moving from mere platformed fame on a dominant profile to cross-platformed influence in which fame and publicity is disseminated across a loose network of profiles.

Generally, advertisers still prefer to be able to track metrics from archivable content in repository format social media but understand the need to capture audiences emerging on transient format social media. As a result, cross-platforming Influencers are becoming a norm, requiring Influencers to manage the distinct platform functions and the cultural norms of each space, their respective dominant Influencers, and their mass of followers.

In my earlier work on how Influencers use selfies commercially,[331] I described how they specifically curate and publish distinct types of selfies for specific social media. For instance, Instagram selfies are the most tasteful and carefully curated to represent one's ideal persona and "best face"; Twitter selfies are other carefully curated shots that did not make the cut for Instagram; while Snapchat selfies are intentionally ugly faces, posed outtakes, and humorous captures to interact more casually with followers and to give the impression of fun. Such split streaming across platforms has become a game and chase for followers per se, inviting them to tune in to Influencers from a "360° angle," calling upon the most loyal of them to track Influencers across all platforms to corroborate facets of an Influencer's persona for consumption.

Attention Economy → Affection Economy

For Influencers, advertised products are malleable and packaged to personify their internet celebrity persona. An Influencer who promotes Product X in one instance may subsequently promote competitor Product Y a few months later, as long as they are able to keep their brand narrative coherent. In other words, the personal brand of the Influencer takes precedence over the corporate brands of the products and services they sell, and this is crucial. Unlike traditional celebrities with their occasional million-dollar endorsements, Influencers depend on a constant stream of smaller sponsored posts, appearances, and endorsements for income. And unlike traditional celebrities who have the capital to commit to just one brand in their lifetime, Influencers must be savvy and malleable enough to take on several brands consecutively, after they have waited out their "embargo" time periods; following a sponsored advertorial, most brands will contractually not allow Influencers to advertise for competitors for a 6- to 12-month window. As a result, Influencers are shifting from the traditional but transient attention economy to the contemporary but more longstanding affection economy.

It pays for Influencers to cultivate the self as a brand and market products through the lens of one's persona, rather than promote products via a corporation's philosophy; Kevin Roberts,[332] CEO of the advertising agency Saatchi & Saatchi, has written about endearing to corporation brands as "Lovemarks," where consumers come to support products out of loyalty to a brand and company rather than out of appreciation or need for the product. Therefore, it is important that clients allow Influencers to personalize and write their own advertorials in their own voice. This is also why such forms of advertorials are especially successful among Influencers in the lifestyle genre, for whom their everyday activities and practices form the backbone of their published content. In other words, it is their lifestyles that are out there on display, for sale, and for emulation. What Influencers are peddling, then, is an economy of affect alongside the economy of attention.

This shift from the attention economy to the affection economy can also be related to Twitter's semiotic update in November 2015, when the platform changed its iconic "stars" into "hearts," and the connotation of "favorites" into likes. In their press release, Twitter wrote:

> *The heart, in contrast, is a universal symbol that resonates across languages, cultures, and time zones. The heart is more expressive, enabling you to convey a range of emotions and easily connect with people. And in our tests, we found that people loved it.*[333]

Just as platforms like Twitter are starting to conflate attention with affection, or viewership with likeability, Influencers in the increasingly saturated industry find themselves required to pursue both short-term spikes in viewer traffic (often through controversies or scandals) alongside long-term investments to grow their loyal base through sustained, sincere interactions.

Quantitative Metrics → Qualitative Impact

Finally, given that the Influencer industry is increasingly saturated and that the shadow economy and black market to boost one's portfolio and impact artificially are becoming more widely available, the value of mere quantitative metrics through subscribers, follower counts, likes, and comments are no longer truthful or sufficient indicators of engagement or impact. Instead, the Influencer industry seems to be regressing from its obsession over quantitative metrics to return to the early days of qualitative impact.

The engagement of most social media profiles can be calculated through the likes of analytic programs provided by digital media companies such as Google or Twitter. Others, like Snapchat, still obscure user metrics on the platform per se, although a variety of third-party tools and dedicated platforms such as Social Blade have emerged to quantify user engagement through their own tools. However, this was not always the case. In the early days of the Influencer industry, "stats" had to be pulled manually by personally visiting each social media page or through self-reportage on platforms like Blogger and WordPress where the backend analytics are not immediately open to the public.

This is still the case for apps like Snapchat, where Influencers have taken to posting screengrabs of how many times each of their stories has been viewed or screenshot to evidence follower engagement. This is no doubt a laborious endeavor considering that stories and their attached metrics are only available for 24 hours, and that Influencers publish multiple stories, several times a day, around the clock. Yet such vernacular practices are just one of several efforts of Influencers to make their impact visible and quantify their standing on a platform that is still relatively new for advertisers.

However, many Influencers have also been observed to be intentionally mystifying their impact, shunning quantifiable data for qualitative anecdotes. Alongside Influencers removing quantified stats from their profiles, I have observed several Influencers posting screengrabs of conversations or feedback

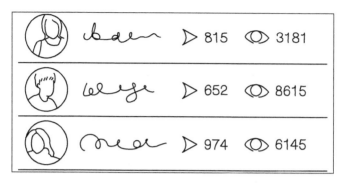

Figure 4.4. Artist's impression of the backend page of a Snapchat profile, featuring metrics such as number of screenshots and number of views. Art produced by LIBA Studio. Used with permission.

with their clients and managers. Some of these are as informal as WhatsApp text messages or direct messages on various platforms, while others are verbatim testimonials on reports churned out by Influencer management companies, personal praise, and fan letters from satisfied followers. We now seem to be reiterating "networked narratives" and "word-of-mouth" selling,[334] which were the primary modes of verification and validation in the earliest days of Influencer commerce. Perhaps as the industry has saturated and professionalized so quickly since it first began in the early 2000s, some Influencers are beginning to opt out of quantitative data cultures and are reverting to yardsticks such as the informal testimonials that garnered them internet fame in the first place.

CONCLUSION

In this chapter, we turned our attention to a specific form of internet celebrity known as Influencers. By reviewing the most recent press coverage and popular commentary on the Influencer industry and accompanying that with some ethnographic research into Influencers in Singapore, we were introduced to the general architecture of the industry, comprising its early structural histories, the place of Influencer agencies and managers as brokers, and the several ways that Influencers generate income. However, as with all competitive economies in society, the increasing benchmarks and saturation of the Influencer industry quietly birthed a shadow economy of black market practices. In this section, we reviewed some of the most common vernacular strategies for gaming the attention economy in Influencer culture, such as the use of bot followers and how platforms push to purge them, the use of hashtag spam to steal attention across interest communities and how platforms enforce shadow bans, and the formation of self-amplification Instagram networks where resources are internally circulated such as Instagram pods and Twitter decks. Given the prevalence of the Influencer industry globally, we then examined some of the key implications of Influencer culture in the areas of economics, legality, culture, and social issues. Finally, as a reflection on the evolution of Influencer culture and social media platforms' adaptations to them, we analyzed five emergent shifts in the industry that newer cohorts of Influencers are taking up slowly but surely.

On the whole, the Influencer industry represents the epitome of internet celebrity, exhibiting the economic, technical, cultural, and social skills required to maintain one's visibility on the internet to create a sustained and viable business. It highlights to us the enduring power of internet celebrities to occupy space on the highly saturated internet, establish meaningful relationships with followers, and demonstrate the impact of young people's creativity and innovation in digital spaces.

POSTFACE

You have just read a book on internet celebrity in a time that can be considered both the Golden Age and the Dark Age of the industry.

For starters, the internet celebrity and Influencer industries are at their most institutionalized, structured, regulated, and organized today, having been honed through various cultural iterations since the mid-2000s. An increasing number of young people are skillfully parlaying their internet fame into full-fledged viable careers, such that dozens of them around the world have become internet-made millionaires. The promise of possibly becoming an internet celebrity, for whatever rhyme or reason, seems a lot more attainable than it was a decade ago. As genres of weird and quirky content on the internet continue to diversify and celebrities emerge out of internet culture for newer (and more unpinnable, random) reasons, it feels as if the culture of internet celebrity is here to stay for a long time to come.

Yet, I have also written this text at a time where the President of one of the most powerful and influential countries in the world is pushing out highly sensational and viral tweets by the day, accumulating more global publicity for his internet celebrity than his presidential duties. Vernacular reactions to the often unprofessional content tweeted by this President are also swiftly garnering fame for many internet users themselves, as they continuously innovate in the ways they appropriate and remix his content for humor and attention, resulting in a shadow economy of competition for visibility and virality with every tweet. The Influencer industry has been plagued by onslaughts of controversies in the last few years, as questions of authenticity, transparency, and sincerity on the internet have been called into question every time a new scandal has erupted. One of my favorite television series, *Black Mirror*, has just launched its fourth season to terrify international audiences with more dark consequences as social media has irrefutably fused with the basic needs of contemporary life.

As such, I write this book as a time capsule bearing snapshots of what the climate of internet celebrity looks like at this point of its trajectory, in the late 2010s. As I eagerly watch cultures of internet celebrity take root, take off, take over, or take flight around the world, I hope that you, like me, will treasure having had this opportunity to grow up and grow old with the internet as it continues to grow on us.

ENDNOTES

1. Turner, Graeme. 2004. *Understanding Celebrity.* Los Angeles: Sage.

2. Geraghty, Christine. 2007. "Re-examining stardom: Questions of texts, bodies and performance." Pp. 98–110 in *Stardom and Celebrity: A Reader,* edited by S. Redmond and S. Holmes. Los Angeles: Sage.

3. Turner, Graeme. 2004. *Understanding Celebrity.* Los Angeles: Sage.

4. Turner, Graeme, France Bonner, and P. David Marshall. 2000. *Fame Games: The Production of Celebrity in Australia.* Cambridge: Cambridge University Press.

5. Rojek, Chris. 2001. *Celebrity.* London: Reaktion Books.

6. Rein, Irving, Philip Kotler, and Martin Stoller. 1997. *High Visibility: The Making and Marketing of Professionals into Celebrities.* New York: McGraw-Hill.

7. Turner, Graeme, France Bonner, and P. David Marshall. 2000. *Fame Games: The Production of Celebrity in Australia.* Cambridge: Cambridge University Press.

8. Turner, Graeme. 2014. *Understanding Celebrity.*
    Los Angeles: Sage, p. 92.

9. Grindstaff, Laura. 2002. *The money shot: Trash,
    class, and the making of TV talk shows.* Chicago:
    University of Chicago Press, pp. 18–19.

10. Grindstaff, Laura. 2002. *The money shot: Trash,
    class, and the making of TV talk shows.* Chicago:
    University of Chicago Press.

11. Turner, Graeme. 2014. *Understanding Celebrity.*
    Los Angeles: Sage.

12. Turner, Graeme. 2014. *Understanding Celebrity.*
    Los Angeles: Sage.

13. Turner, Graeme. 2014. *Understanding Celebrity.*
    Los Angeles: Sage.

14. Thomas, Bronwen, and Julia Round. 2014.
    "Introduction." Pp. 1–9 in *Real Lives, Celebrity
    Stories: Narratives of Ordinary and Extraordinary
    People Across Media,* edited by B. Thomas, and
    J. Round. London: Bloomsbury.

15. Batty, Craig. 2014. "Me and you and everyone we
    know: The centrality of character in understanding
    media texts." Pp. 35–56 in *Real Lives, Celebrity
    Stories: Narratives of Ordinary and Extraordinary
    People Across Media,* edited by B. Thomas and
    J. Round. London: Bloomsbury.

16. Hill, Annette. 2005. *Reality TV: Audiences and
    popular factual television.* London: Routledge,
    p. 178.

17. Ouellette, Laurie, and James Hay. 2008. *Better Living
    through Reality TV.* Oxford: Blackwell, pp. 101–102.

18. Horton, Donald, and Wohl, R. Richard. 1956. "Mass communication and para- social interaction." *Psychiatry* 19(3): 215–229. Republished in *Particip@tions 3(1)*. Retrieved June 15, 2013 (http://www.aber.ac.uk/media/Modules/TF33120/horton_and_wohl_1956.html)

19. Rojek, Chris. 2001. *Celebrity.* London: Reaktion Books, p. 52.

20. Turner, Graeme. 2004. *Understanding Celebrity.* Los Angeles: Sage.

21. Marshall, P. David. 2010. "The promotion and presentation of the self: Celebrity as marker of presentational media." *Celebrity Studies* 1(1): 45.

22. Bennett, James. 2011. *Television Personalities: Stardom and the Small Screen.* London: Routledge.

23. Turner, Graeme. 2004. *Understanding Celebrity.* Los Angeles: Sage.

24. Burgess, Jean, and Joshua Green. 2009. *YouTube: Online Video and Participatory Culture.* Cambridge: Polity Press.

25. Marwick, Alice E., and danah boyd. 2010. "I tweet honestly, I tweet passionately: Twitter users, context collapse, and the imagined audience." *New Media & Society* 13(1): 114–133.

26. Senft, Theresa M. 2008. *Camgirls: Celebrity & Community in the Age of Social Networks.* New York: Peter Lang Publishers.

27. Senft, Theresa M. 2008. *Camgirls: Celebrity & Community in the Age of Social Networks.* New York: Peter Lang Publishers, p. 25.

28. Senft, Theresa M. 2008. *Camgirls: Celebrity & Community in the Age of Social Networks*. New York: Peter Lang Publishers, p. 8.

29. Senft, Theresa M. 2008. *Camgirls: Celebrity & Community in the Age of Social Networks*. New York: Peter Lang Publishers, pp. 25–26, 45–46, 116.

30. Marwick, Alice. 2013. *Status Update: Celebrity, Publicity and Branding in the Social Media Age*. New Haven: Yale University Press.

31. Marwick, Alice. 2013. *Status Update: Celebrity, Publicity and Branding in the Social Media Age*. New Haven: Yale University Press, p. 114.

32. Marwick, Alice. 2013. *Status Update: Celebrity, Publicity and Branding in the Social Media Age*. New Haven: Yale University Press, pp. 15–16.

33. Marwick, Alice. 2013. *Status Update: Celebrity, Publicity and Branding in the Social Media Age*. New Haven: Yale University Press, pp. 116, 121–123.

34. Marwick, Alice. 2013. *Status Update: Celebrity, Publicity and Branding in the Social Media Age*. New Haven: Yale University Press, pp. 208, 117.

35. Abidin, Crystal. 2016a. "Visibility labour: Engaging with Influencers' fashion brands and #OOTD advertorial campaigns on Instagram." *Media International Australia* 161(1): 86–100.

36. Duffy, Brooke Erin. 2016. "The romance of work: Gender and aspirational labour in the digital culture industries." *International Journal of Cultural Studies* 19(4): 441–457.

37. Wissinger, Elizabeth. 2015. *This Year's Model: Fashion, Media, and the Making of Glamour*. New York: NYU Press.

38. Booth, Norman, and Julie Ann Matic. 2011. "Mapping and leveraging influencers in social media to shape corporate brand perceptions." *Corporate Communications: An International Journal* 16(3): 184–191.

39. Page, Ruth. 2012. "The linguistics of self-branding and micro-celebrity in Twitter: The role of hashtags." *Discourse & Communication* 6(2): 181–201.

40. McMillan Cottom, Tressie. 2015. "'Who do you think you are?': When marginality meets academic microcelebrity." *Ada: A Journal of Gender, New Media, and Technology* 7.

41. Tufeci, Zeynep. 2013. "'Not this one': Social movements, the attention economy, and microcelebrity networked activism." *American Behavioral Scientist* 57(7): 848–870.

42. Guarriello, Nicholas-Brie. 2017. "And the world will turn to cash: Pokémon GO Fanart & the convergence of affective/monetary labor on Tumblr and Patreon." *Affective Politics of Social Media Conference,* University of Tartu, 12–13 October 2017.

43. Meng, Di. 2014. "Camera girl 2.0: A study of Chinese women's online visual representation in the age of individualization." PhD Thesis, School of Creative Media, City University of Hong Kong.

44. Wang, Yuejia. 2017. "'We are famous on the Internet': A study of the Chinese phenomenon of Wanghong." MA Thesis, Department of Linguistic, Literary and Aesthetic Studies, University of Bergen.

45. Rahmawan, Detta. 2013. "Selebtwits: Micro-celebrity practitioners in Indonesian Twittersphere." *SSRN* August 28, 2013.

46. García-Rapp, Florencia, and Carles. Roca-Cuberes. 2017. "Being an online celebrity: Norms and expectations of YouTube's beauty community." *First Monday* 22(7).

47. Gibbs, Martin, James Meese, Michael Arnold, Bjorn Nansen, and Marcus Carter. 2015. "#Funeral and Instagram: Death, social media, and platform vernacular." *Information, Communication & Society* 18(3): 255–268.

48. Hearn, Alison, and Stephanie Schoenhoff. 2015. "From celebrity to influencer: Tracing the diffusion of celebrity value across the data stream." Pp. 194–212 in *A Companion to Celebrity*, edited by P. David Marshall and Sean Redmond. John Wiley & Sons.

49. Senft, Theresa M. 2008. *Camgirls: Celebrity & Community in the Age of Social Networks*. New York: Peter Lang Publishers.

50. Marwick, Alice. 2013. *Status Update: Celebrity, Publicity and Branding in the Social Media Age.* New Haven: Yale University Press.

51. Abidin, Crystal, and Eric C. Thompson. 2012. "Buymylife.com: Cyberfemininities and commercial intimacy in blogshops." *Women's Studies International Forum* 35(6): 467–477.

52. Abidin, Crystal. 2014. "#In$tagLam: Instagram as a repository of taste, a brimming marketplace, a war of eyeballs." Pp. 119–128 in *Mobile Media Making in the Age of Smartphones,* edited by Marsha Berry and Max Schleser. New York: Palgrave Pivot.

53. Abidin, Crystal. 2016b. "Aren't these just young, rich women doing vain things online?: Influencer selfies as subversive frivolity." *Social Media + Society* 2(2): 1–17.

54. Abidin, Crystal. 2016a. "Visibility labour: Engaging with Influencers' fashion brands and #OOTD advertorial campaigns on Instagram." *Media International Australia* 161(1): 86–100.

55. Abidin, Crystal. 2015. "Micromicrocelebrity: Branding babies on the Internet." *M/C Journal* 18(5).

56. Abidin, Crystal. 2017. "#familygoals: Family Influencers, calibrated amateurism, and justifying young digital labour." *Social Media + Society* 3(2): 1–15.

57. Abidin, Crystal. 2017. "#familygoals: Family Influencers, calibrated amateurism, and justifying young digital labour." *Social Media + Society* 3(2): 1–15.

58. Abidin, Crystal. 2017. "#familygoals: Family Influencers, calibrated amateurism, and justifying young digital labour." *Social Media + Society* 3(2): 1–15.

59. The Late Late Show with James Corden. 2018. "About." *YouTube.com.* Last accessed January 21, 2018 from https://www.youtube.com/user/TheLateLateShow/about

60. Robehmed, Natalie. 2016. "Inside the business of Kardashian-Jenner Instagram endorsements." *Forbes,* November 16. Last accessed January 21, 2018 from https://www.forbes.com/sites/natalierobehmed/2016/11/16/inside-the-business-of-celebrity-instagram-endorsements/#33178b8c5724

61. Minton, Melissa. 2017. "Chrissy Teigen asked Twitter for help finding ingredients for banana bread." *Teen Vogue,* September 21. Last accessed January 21, 2018, from https://www.teenvogue.com/story/chrissy-teigen-twitter-bananas

62. Abidin, Crystal. 2017b. "Vote for my selfie: Politician selfies as charismatic engagement." Pp. 75–87 in *Selfie Citizenship*, edited by Adi Kuntsman. London: Palgrave Pivot.

63. Laurent, Dheepthika. 2017. "The social media election: French candidates show their funny side." *France 24*, 20 April. Last accessed January 21, 2018 from http://www.france24.com/en/mediawatch/20170420-cocial-media-election-french-candidates-show-funny-side

64. Marwick, Alice. 2013. *Status Update: Celebrity, Publicity and Branding in the Social Media Age*. New Haven: Yale University Press, pp.133–148.

65. Senft, Theresa M. 2008. *Camgirls: Celebrity & Community in the Age of Social Networks*. New York: Peter Lang Publishers, pp. 25–26.

66. Bourdieu, Pierre. 1986. "The forms of capital." Pp. 241–258 in *Handbook of Theory and Research for the Sociology of Education,* edited by Richardson, J. Westport, CT: Greenwood.

67. Bourdieu, Pierre. 1986. "The forms of capital." Pp. 241–258 in *Handbook of Theory and Research for the Sociology of Education,* edited by Richardson, J. Westport, CT: Greenwood.

68. Kelly, Heather. 2012. "What's next for the Rich Kids of Instagram?" *CNN.com,* August 19. Last accessed January 8, 2018 from http://edition.cnn.com/2012/08/17/tech/web/rich-kids-of-instagram/index.html

69. rkoi. 2018. "Rich Kids Of…" *Instagram.com*. Last accessed January 8, 2018 from https://www.instagram.com/rkoi/

70. Griffiths, Josie. 2017. "Arab Bling: It's always summer for the Rich Kids of Dubai… and these snaps of their amazing lifestyle will make you jealous." *The Sun,* April 21. Last accessed January 8, 2018 from https://www.thesun.co.uk/living/3383228/summer-rich-kids-dubai/

71. Millington, Alison. 2017a. "How Instagarm's 'Rich Kids of Hong Kong' spend their fortunes." *Business Insider,* June 14. Last accessed January 8, 2018 from https://www.businessinsider.com.au/how-instagram-rich-kids-of-hong-kong-spend-their-fortunes-2017-6?_ga=2.258967114.1780322250.1515415879-1620979888.1515415879&r=UK&IR=T

72. Millington, Alison. 2017b. "How Instagram's 'Rich Kids of Switzerland' spend their fortunes." *This Is Insider,* July 11. Last accessed January 8, 2018 from http://www.thisisinsider.com/how-instagrams-rich-kids-of-switzerland-spend-their-fortunes-2017-7

73. Cliff, Martha. 2017. "Bespoke cars, endless holidays and some VERY cheeky selfies: A few decades after the fall of Europe's hardest-line communist regime, The Rich Kids of Tirana flaunt their enviable fortune online." *Daily Mail,* October 24. Last accessed January 8, 2018 from http://www.dailymail.co.uk/femail/article-5009003/The-Rich-Kids-Tirana-flaunt-fortune-online.html

74. Brennan, Siofra. 2016. "Houses decked in gold, collecting Louboutins like coupons and spraying money from a GUN! Are the rich kids of Nigeria the most outrageous yet with their lavish displays of wealth?" *Daily Mail,* October 20. Last accessed January 8, 2018 from http://www.dailymail.co.uk/femail/article-3855038/Rich-kids-Nigeria-shade-lavish-display-wealth.html

75. Lakritz, Talia. 2017. "How Instagram's 'Rich Kids of Vietnam' spend their fortunes." *Business Insider,* July 18. Last accessed January 8, 2018 from http://www.businessinsider.com/rich-kids-of-instagram-vietnam-2017-7?IR=T

76. The Creator of Rich Kids of Instagram, and Maya Sloan. 2014. Rich Kids of Instagram: A Novel. New York: Gallery Books.

77. E News. 2018. "Rich Kids of Beverly Hills." *Eonline. com,* n.d. Last accessed January 8, 2018 from http://www.eonline.com/au/shows/rich_kids_of_beverly_hills

78. Channel 4. 2018. "Rich Kids of Instagram." *Channel4.com,* n.d. Last accessed January 8, 2018 from http://www.channel4.com/programmes/rich-kids-of-instagram

79. Squier, Chem. 2014. "Have the 'Rich Kids of Instagram' started shitting themselves?" *Vice.com,* June 23. Last accessed January 8, 2018 from https://www.vice.com/en_us/article/mv59aq/rich-kids-of-instagram-lord-aleem-arson

80. richkidsof. 2018. "Rich Kids Of Instagram." *Instagram.com.* Last accessed January 8, 2018 from https://www.instagram.com/richkidsof/

81. Bourdieu, Pierre. 1986. "The forms of capital." Pp. 241–258 in *Handbook of Theory and Research for the Sociology of Education,* edited by Richardson, J. Westport, CT: Greenwood.

82. Crenshaw, Kimberlé. 1989. "Demarginalizing the intersection of race and sex: A black feminist critique of antidiscrimination doctrine, feminist theory and

antiracist politics." *University of Chicago Legal Forum*, Vol. 1989, Article 8.

83. Yuka Kinoshita. 2018. "Yuka Kinoshita." *YouTube. com*. Last accessed January 9, 2018 from https://www.youtube.com/user/kinoyuu0204/about

84. Yuka Kinoshita. 2015. "Kinoshita Yuka [OoGui Eater] 4 buckets of KFC, 48 pieces of chicken!!" *YouTube.com*, December 30. Last accessed January 9, 2018 from https://www.youtube.com/watch?v=-dxqlXPyDl4

85. Said, Edward W. 1978. *Orientalism*. Routledge & Kegan Paul: London and Henley.

86. wishcrys. 2016. "Pen-Pineapple-Apple-Pen and the lifecycle of internet virality." *wishcrys.com*, September 29. Last accessed February 8, 2018 from https://wishcrys.com/2016/09/29/pen-pineapple-apple-pen-and-the-lifecycle-of-internet-virality/

87. wishcrys. 2017. "Meitu Xiuxiu, cultural diffusion, and Asia exotica." *wishcrys.com*, January 18. Last accessed February 8, 2018 from https://wishcrys.com/2017/01/19/meituxiuxiu-cultural-diffusion-and-asia-exotica/

88. Yuka Kinoshita. 2018. "Yuka Kinoshita." *YouTube. com*. Last accessed January 9, 2018 from https://www.youtube.com/user/kinoyuu0204/about

89. Blattberg, Eric. 2015. "The demographics of YouTube, in 5 charts." *Digiday.com*, April 24. Last accessed January 9, 2018 from https://digiday.com/media/demographics-youtube-5-charts/

90. Socialbakers. 2018a. "Entertainment YouTube statistics – Online Show." *Socialbakers.com*. Last

accessed January 9, 2018 from https://www.
socialbakers.com/statistics/youtube/channels/
entertainment/online-show/

91. Social Blade. 2018a. "Top 250 YouTubers
    entertainment channels sorted by video views."
    Socialblade.com. Last accessed January 9, 2018
    from https://socialblade.com/youtube/top/category/
    entertainment/mostviewed

92. さぁや saaya. 2018. "About." *YouTube.com.* Last
    accessed January 9, 2018 from https://www.youtube.
    com/channel/UC69xoWl5-Y3m-oRFTORIbKw/
    about

93. sasakiasahi. 2018. "About." *YouTube.com.* Last
    accessed January 9, 2018 from https://www.youtube.
    com/user/sasakiasahi/about

94. SekineRisa. 2018. "About." *YouTube.com.* Last
    accessed January 9, 2018 from https://www.
    youtube.com/user/SekineRisa/about

95. Social Blade. 2018b. "Top 250 YouTubers in Japan
    sorted by subscribers." *Socialblade.com.* Last
    accessed January 9, 2018 from https://socialblade.
    com/youtube/top/country/jp/mostsubscribed

96. Universal Music Japan. 2018. "About." *YouTube.
    com.* Last accessed January 17, 2018 from https://
    www.youtube.com/user/universalmusicjapan/about

97. AKB48. 2018. "About." *YouTube.com.* Last accessed
    January 17, 2018 from https://www.youtube.com/
    user/AKB48/about

98. Kan & Aki's CHANNEL. 2018. "About." *YouTube.
    com.* Last accessed January 17, 2018 from https://
    www.youtube.com/user/potemi926/about

99. がっちゃんねる★ TheGacchannel. 2018. "About." *YouTube.com*. Last accessed January 17, 2018 from https://www.youtube.com/user/TheGacchannel/about

100. 兄者弟者. 2018. "About." *YouTube.com*. Last accessed January 17, 2018 from https://www.youtube.com/user/norunine/about

101. HikakinTV. 2018. "About." *YouTube.com*. Last accessed January 17, 2018 from https://www.youtube.com/user/HikakinTV/about

102. Socialbakers. 2018b. "YouTube statistics for Japan." *Socialbakers.com*. Last accessed January 9, 2018 from https://www.socialbakers.com/statistics/youtube/channels/japan/

103. Yardi, Sarita. 2010. "A theory of technical capital." *TMSP Workshop, Georgia Institute of Technology*. Last accessed January 17, 2018 from https://pdfs.semanticscholar.org/717b/195de57ca043ef85d54a04260297e1dc7331.pdf

104. Hayhoe, Simon, Kris Roger, Sebastiaan Eldritch-Böersen, and Linda Kelland. 2015. "Developing Inclusive Technical Capital beyond the Disabled Students' Allowance in England." *Social Inclusion, 3*(6): 29–41.

105. jwcfree. 2018. "About." *YouTube.com*. Last accessed January 16, 2018 from https://www.youtube.com/user/jwcfree/about

106. jwcfree. 2008. "(Movie Theme) Pirates Of The Caribbean – Sungha Jung." *YouTube.com*, October 12. Last accessed January 17, 2018 from https://www.youtube.com/watch?v=g5WB-p-QBJc

107. Ignacio, Angela V. 2014. "Boy wonder: The magic of Sungha Jung's music." *Inquirer.net,* August 23.

Last accessed January 16, 2018 from http://lifestyle.
inquirer.net/169400/boy-wonder-the-magic-of-
sungha-jungs-music/

108. Sungha Jung. 2018a. "shop & bbs." *Sunghajung.
com.* Last accessed January 16, 2018 from http://
www.sunghajung.com/new_shop

109. Tham, Chastina, and Kyra Patricia Tayer. 2016.
"Exclusive Interview: 5 questions with Sungha Jung."
The Urban Wire, June 30. Last accessed January 16,
2018 from https://www.theurbanwire.com/2016/06/
exclusive-interview-5-questions-with-sungha-jung/

110. Sungha Jung. 2018b. "About." *Sunghajung.com.*
Last accessed January 16, 2018 from http://www.
sunghajung.com/about

111. Pulley, Anna. 2017. "'Acoustic Uprising' documentary
explores fingerstyle's rise to prominence." *Acoustic
Guitar,* September 17. Last accessed January 16,
2018 from http://acousticguitar.com/acoustic-
uprising-documentary-explores-fingerstyles-rise-to-
prominence/

112. Lavoie, Stephen. 2016. "Sungha Jung: Growing up
on YouTube." *Rappler,* 10 February. Last accessed
January 16, 2018 from https://www.rappler.com/
entertainment/music/121988-sungha-jung-guitar-
finger-style-youtube-star

113. Ortiz, Meann. 2013. "Sungha Jung: From YouTube
to live stage." *GMA News Online,* July 5. Last
accessed January 16, 2018 from http://www.
gmanetwork.com/news/lifestyle/content/316126/
sungha-jung-from-youtube-to-live-stage/story/

114. theofficialsunghajung. 2018. "정성하 SUNGHA
JUNG." *Instagram.com.* Last accessed January 16,

2018 from https://www.instagram.com/
theofficialsunghajung/?hl=en

115. Korea Boo. 2017. "This Chinese YouTuber is going
     viral for cooking food using only office supplies."
     Korea Boo, April 20. Last accessed January 16,
     2018 from https://www.koreaboo.com/buzz/
     chinese-youtuber-creates-different-kinds-of-food-
     at-work-using-supplies-you-could-find-around-the-
     office/

116. Tay, Samantha. 2017. "From burning off her
     brows to meeting Jack Ma – All in a day's work
     for Me Yeah." *Vulcan Post,* November 7. Last
     accessed January 16, 2018 from https://vulcanpost.
     com/624744/ms-yeah-singapore-office-chef/

117. AsiaOne. 2017. "'The Office Chef' Ms Yeah takes
     lunches to a whole new level." *AsiaOne,* August
     12. Last accessed January 16, 2018 from http://
     www.asiaone.com/food/office-chef-ms-yeah-takes-
     lunches-whole-new-level

118. Reuters. 2017. "China's 'office chef' a hit with
     online foodies." *Reuters,* September 26. Last
     accessed January 16, 2018 from https://www.
     reuters.com/article/us-china-internet-celebrity/
     chinas-office-chef-a-hit-with-online-foodies-
     idUSKCN1C10W8

119. Tay, Samantha. 2017. "From burning off her
     brows to meeting Jack Ma – All in a day's work
     for Me Yeah." *Vulcan Post,* November 7. Last
     accessed January 16, 2018 from https://vulcanpost.
     com/624744/ms-yeah-singapore-office-chef/

120. Ang, Tian Tian. 2017. "China's Internet sensation,
     the office chef, is branching out to stay relevant."

The New Paper, October 31. Last accessed
January 16, 2018 from http://www.tnp.sg/lifestyle/
others/big-plans-works-chinas-office-chef-internet-
sensation

121. Content Summit. 2017. "Ms Yeah: China's latest
     Internet sensation." *Content Summit 2017.*
     Last accessed January 16, 2018 from https://
     contentsummit.asia/speaker/ms-yeah/

122. Reuters. 2017. "China's 'office chef' a hit with
     online foodies." *Reuters,* September 26. Last
     accessed January 16, 2018 from https://www.
     reuters.com/article/us-china-internet-celebrity/
     chinas-office-chef-a-hit-with-online-foodies-
     idUSKCN1C10W8

123. Zhuang, Pinghui. 2017. "The global reach of a
     quirky office chef as China's internet celebrity
     economy booms." *South China Morning Post,*
     July 29. Last accessed January 16, 2018 from
     http://www.scmp.com/news/china/society/article/
     2104371/global-reach-quirky-office-chef-chinas-
     internet-celebrity-economy

124. Sochocki, Trevor. 2017. "How to cook meals using
     only everyday office equipment." *BBC,* August 14.
     Last accessed January 16, 2018 from http://www.
     bbc.com/capital/story/20170811-how-to-cook-
     meals-using-only-everyday-office-equipment

125. Zhang, Ge, and Larissa Hjorth. 2017. "Live-
     streaming, games and politics of gender
     performance: The case of *Nüzhubo* in China."
     *Convergence: The International Journal of Research
     into New Media Technologies* 1–17. Online first
     last accessed February 8, 2018 from http://journals.
     sagepub.com/doi/10.1177/1354856517738160

126. Zhuang, Pinghui. 2017. "The global reach of a quirky office chef as China's internet celebrity economy booms." *South China Morning Post,* July 29. Last accessed January 16, 2018 from http://www.scmp.com/news/china/society/article/ 2104371/global-reach-quirky-office-chef-chinas-internet-celebrity-economy

127. Sochocki, Trevor. 2017. "How to cook meals using only everyday office equipment." *BBC,* August 14. Last accessed January 16, 2018 from http://www. bbc.com/capital/story/20170811-how-to-cook-meals-using-only-everyday-office-equipment

128. Chen, Siyi. 2017. "How to cook elaborate dishes using everyday office supplies – like China's newest internet star." *Quartzy,* April 27. Last accessed January 16, 2018 from https://quartzy. qz.com/968293/ms-yeah-chinas-newest-internet-star-cooks-elaborate-dishes-with-everyday-office-supplies/

129. Tay, Samantha. 2017. "From burning off her brows to meeting Jack Ma – All in a day's work for Me Yeah." *Vulcan Post,* November 7. Last accessed January 16, 2018 from https://vulcanpost. com/624744/ms-yeah-singapore-office-chef/

130. Ang, Tian Tian. 2017. "China's Internet sensation, the office chef, is branching out to stay relevant." *The New Paper,* October 31. Last accessed January 16, 2018 from http://www.tnp.sg/lifestyle/others/big-plans-works-chinas-office-chef-internet-sensation

131. Bourdieu, Pierre. 1986. "The forms of capital." Pp. 241–258 in *Handbook of Theory and Research for the Sociology of Education,* edited by Richardson, J. Westport, CT: Greenwood.

132. Lauraiz. 2018. "Laura Izumikawa." *Instagram.com.* Last accessed January 17, 2018 from https://www. instagram.com/lauraiz/

133. Bologna, Caroline. 2016. "This baby has no idea she's the queen of dress-up while she naps." *Huffington Post,* August 25. Last accessed January 16, 2018 from http://www.huffingtonpost.com.au/ entry/this-baby-has-no-idea-shes-the-queen-of-dress-up-while-she-naps_us_57bda18ee4b03d51368bbc09

134. Bologna, Caroline. 2017. "The adorable napping baby whose dress-up adventures went viral has her own book now." *Huffington Post,* November 9. Last accessed January 16, 2018 from http://www. huffingtonpost.com.au/entry/the-adorable-napping-baby-whose-dress-up-adventures-went-viral-has-her-own-book-now_us_5a0346fee4b03deac08a9446

135. Bologna, Caroline. 2016. "This baby has no idea she's the queen of dress-up while she naps." *Huffington Post,* August 25. Last accessed January 16, 2018 from http://www.huffingtonpost.com.au/ entry/this-baby-has-no-idea-shes-the-queen-of-dress-up-while-she-naps_us_57bda18ee4b03d51368bbc09

136. Bologna, Caroline. 2017. "The adorable napping baby whose dress-up adventures went viral has her own book now." *Huffington Post,* November 9. Last accessed January 16, 2018 from http://www. huffingtonpost.com.au/entry/the-adorable-napping-baby-whose-dress-up-adventures-went-viral-has-her-own-book-now_us_5a0346fee4b03deac08a9446

137. Laura Iz. 2018b. "Shop." *Lauraiz.com.* Last accessed January 17, 2018 from http://lauraiz.com/shop/

138. Laura Iz. 2018a. "FAQ." *Lauraiz.com.* Last accessed January 17, 2018 from http://lauraiz.com/faq/

139. Lauraiz. 2018. "Laura Izumikawa." Instagram.com. Last accessed 17 January 2018 from https://www. instagram.com/lauraiz/

140. Laura Iz. 2018a. "FAQ." Lauraiz.com. Last accessed 17 January 2018 from http://lauraiz.com/faq/

141. CharlieHannenmaNewson6. 2016. Michelle Dobyne interview. *Facebook.com*, n.d. Last accessed April 5, 2016 from https://www. facebook.com/CharlieHannemaNewson6/ videos/935316736504685/ (since removed).

142. CrazyLaughAction. 2012. "Antoine Dodson 'Hide yo Kids, Hide Yo Wife' interview (Original)." *YouTube. com*, April 11. Last accessed January 6, 2018 from https://www.youtube.com/watch?v=EzNhaLUT520 (copy of video; original since untraceable).

143. McCarter, Mark. 2012. "Antoine Dodson takes next step in career, releasing new music video." *AL. com*, February 8. Last accessed January 6, 2018 from http://blog.al.com/breaking/2012/02/antoine_ dodson_takes_next_step.html

144. Molloy, Tim. 2011. "Antoine Dodson, of 'Bed Intruder' fame, gets reality show pilot." *The Wrap*, January 23. Last accessed January 6, 2018 from https://www.thewrap.com/antoine-dodson-bed-intruder-fame-gets-reality-show-pilot-24107/

145. Vanessa C. 2012. "Ain't nobody got time for that!-original." *YouTube.com*, October 28. Last accessed January 6, 2018 from https://www.youtube.com/ watch?v=zGxwbhkDjZM (copy of video; original since untraceable)

146. Shortline Dental. 2013. "Sweet Brown toothache? Ain't nobody got time for that!" *YouTube.com*,

February 6. Last accessed January 6, 2018
from https://www.youtube.com/watch?v=
oSTy4qVw9yQ

147. Riddell, Marlena. 2013. "Tyler Perry casts Sweet
      Brown in a new Madea movie: Apparently America
      has time for this." *Chicago Now,* February 18.
      Last accessed January 6, 2018 from http://www.
      chicagonow.com/chicago-indie-movie-scene/2013/02/
      tyler-perry-casts-sweet-brown-in-new-madea-movie-
      apparently-america-has-time-for-this/

148. VisualiveTV. 2013. "Dead giveaway! Black man
      rescues missing white teens. Charles Ramsey
      interview. Classic." *YouTube.com,* May 6. Last
      accessed January 6, 2018 from https://www.
      youtube.com/watch?v=SdtCEaxfT38 (copy of
      video; original since untraceable).

149. VisualiveTV. 2013. "Dead giveaway! Black man
      rescues missing white teens. Charles Ramsey
      interview. Classic." *YouTube.com,* May 6. Last
      accessed January 6, 2018 from https://www.
      youtube.com/watch?v=SdtCEaxfT38 (copy of
      video; original since untraceable).

150. Power 96. 2016. "'Like a tornado girl!' Animated
      eyewitness account goes viral." *power96.radio.com,*
      June 11. Last accessed January 6, 2018 from http://
      power96.radio.com/2015/06/11/like-a-tornado-girl-
      animated-eyewitness-account-goes-viral/

151. Steel, Catherine Knight. 2013. "Shaking off the
      'Other': Appropriation of marginalized cultures
      and the 'Harlem Shake'." *Selected Papers of Internet
      Research 4.0.* Last accessed January 18, 2018 from
      https://spir.aoir.org/index.php/spir/article/view/838/
      pdf

152. Schilling, Dave. 2016. "Viral video news memes bring fame – but still feel almost racist." *The Guardian,* January 15. Last accessed January 6, 2018 from https://www.theguardian.com/tv-and-radio/2016/jan/14/viral-video-news-memes-michelle-dobyne-antoine-dodson-bed-intruder

153. Blay, Zeba. 2016. "Why do we laugh at viral stars like Michelle Dobyne and Antoine Dodson?" *Huffington Post,* January 16. Last accessed January 6, 2018 from http://www.huffingtonpost.com.au/entry/why-do-we-laugh-at-viral-stars-like-michelle-dobyne-and-antoine-dodson_us_5697c804e4b0b4e b759d6570?section=australia

154. Parker, Asha. 2016. "Will the memeification and autotuning of news interviews with poor and working-class people of color ever end?" *Salon.com,* January 15. Last accessed January 6, 2018 from https://www.salon.com/2016/01/15/will_the_memeification_and_autotuning_of_news_interviews_with_poor_and_working_class_people_of_color_ever_end/

155. Farley, Megan. 2016. "Tulsa viral video star: Life after 15 minutes of fame." *News On 6,* April 1. Last accessed January 6, 2018 from http://www.newson6.com/story/31616553/tulsa-viral-video-star-life-after-15-minutes-of-fame

156. AnnieChangNewsOn6. 2016. Michelle Dobyne interview. *Facebook.com*, n.d. Last accessed April 5, 2016 from https://www.facebook.com/AnnieChangNewsOn6/videos/429305640527352/ (since removed).

157. Dickey, Megan Rose. 2013. "'Ain't nobody got time for that' viral-video star does have time to sue

Apple." *Business Insider,* March 13. Last accessed
January 6, 2018 from https://www.businessinsider.
com.au/sweet-brown-apple-lawsuit-2013-3

158. Huffington Post. 2013. "Antoine Dodson says
he is 'No Longer Into Homosexuality' and now
wants a wife (VIDEO)." *Huffington Post,* March 5.
Last accessed January 6, 2018 from https://www.
huffingtonpost.com/2013/05/03/antoine-dodson-no-
longer-into-homosexuality-gay_n_3209170.html

159. Milner, Ryan M. 2016. *The World Made Meme:
Public Conversations and Participatory Media.*
Cambridge, Massachusetts: MIT Press, p. 3.

160. Milner, Ryan M. 2016. *The World Made Meme:
Public Conversations and Participatory Media.*
Cambridge, Massachusetts: MIT Press, p. 3.

161. Milner, Ryan M. 2016. *The World Made Meme:
Public Conversations and Participatory Media.*
Cambridge, Massachusetts: MIT Press, p. 189.

162. Milner, Ryan M. 2016. *The World Made Meme:
Public Conversations and Participatory Media.*
Cambridge, Massachusetts: MIT Press, pp 185–190.

163. Hayden, Erik. 2012. "Internet, meet 'Ridiculously
Photogenic Guy'." *Time,* April 6. Last accessed
January 10, 2018 from http://newsfeed.time.
com/2012/04/06/internet-meet-ridiculously-
photogenic-guy/

164. Haberman, Stephanie. 2012. "Ridiculously
Photogenic Guy answers questions on Reddit."
Mashable Australia, April 17. Last accessed January
10, 2018 from http://mashable.com/2012/04/16/
ridiculously-photogenic-guy-answers-questions-on-
reddit/#O24qV2LZakq4

165. Robertson, Matt. 2014. "This is the man who
     made Grumpy Cat rich." *Mashable Australia,* June
     4. Last accessed January 10, 2018 from http://
     mashable.com/2014/06/04/ben-lashes-video-
     profile/#tG5H3GrwauqE

166. Robertson, Matt. 2014. "This is the man who
     made Grumpy Cat rich." *Mashable Australia,* June
     4. Last accessed January 10, 2018 from http://
     mashable.com/2014/06/04/ben-lashes-video-
     profile/#tG5H3GrwauqE

167. Milner, Ryan M. 2016. *The World Made Meme:
     Public Conversations and Participatory Media.*
     Cambridge, Massachusetts: MIT Press, p. 195.

168. Contrera, Jessica. 2015. "Being Bad Luck Brian:
     When the meme that made you famous starts
     to fade away." *The Washington Post,* January 5.
     Last accessed January 9, 2018 from https://www.
     washingtonpost.com/lifestyle/style/being-bad-luck-
     brian-when-the-meme-that-made-you-famous-
     starts-to-fade-away/2015/01/05/07cbf6ac-907c-
     11e4-a412-4b735edc7175_story.html?utm_term=.
     fb3e1b53ddda

169. Contrera, Jessica. 2015. "Being Bad Luck Brian:
     When the meme that made you famous starts
     to fade away." *The Washington Post,* January 5.
     Last accessed January 9, 2018 from https://www.
     washingtonpost.com/lifestyle/style/being-bad-luck-
     brian-when-the-meme-that-made-you-famous-starts-
     to-fade-away/2015/01/05/07cbf6ac-907c-11e4-a412-
     4b735edc7175_story.html?utm_term=.fb3e1b53ddda

170. Contrera, Jessica. 2015. "Being Bad Luck Brian:
     When the meme that made you famous starts
     to fade away." *The Washington Post,* January 5.

Last accessed January 9, 2018 from https://www.
washingtonpost.com/lifestyle/style/being-bad-luck-
brian-when-the-meme-that-made-you-famous-
starts-to-fade-away/2015/01/05/07cbf6ac-907c-
11e4-a412-4b735edc7175_story.html?utm_term=.
fb3e1b53ddda

171. Know Your Meme. 2018a. "Success kid / I hate
     sandcastles." *Knowyourmeme.com.* Last accessed
     January 9, 2018 from http://knowyourmeme.com/
     memes/success-kid-i-hate-sandcastles

172. Earl, Jennifer. 2016. "What happened to the boy in
     viral 'Success Kid' meme – 9 years later." *CBS News,*
     December 14. Last accessed January 9, 2018 from
     https://www.cbsnews.com/news/what-happened-
     to-success-kid-sammy-griner-viral-meme-9-years-
     later/

173. Silverman, Matt. 2015. "Success Kid's dad needs
     your help getting a new kidney." *The Daily Dot,*
     April13. Last accessed January 9, 2018 from
     https://www.dailydot.com/news/success-kid-dad-
     kidney-transplant/

174. Nahon, Karine, and Jeff Hemsley. 2013. *Going
     Viral.* Cambridge: Polity Press, pp. 199–201.

175. Shontell, Alyson. 2014. "This 29-year-old was a
     waitress — then she got a cat with dwarfism, quit
     her job, and became a multi-millionaire." *Business
     Insider,* December 8. Last accessed January
     15, 2018 from http://www.businessinsider.com/
     meet-grumpy-cats-owner-tabetha-bundesen-2014-
     12/?r=AU&IR=T

176. Shontell, Alyson. 2014. "This 29-year-old was a
     waitress — then she got a cat with dwarfism, quit

her job, and became a multi-millionaire." *Business Insider,* December 8. Last accessed January 15, 2018 from http://www.businessinsider.com/ meet-grumpy-cats-owner-tabetha-bundesen-2014-12/?r=AU&IR=T

177. Fuchs, Christian. 2017. The Information Economy and the Labor Theory of Value. *International Journal of Political Economy*, 46(1): 65–89.

178. realgrumpycat. 2018. "Grumpy Cat." *Instagram. com.* Last accessed January 15, 2018 from https:// www.instagram.com/realgrumpycat/?hl=en

179. The Official Grumpy Cat. 2018. "Home." *Facebook. com.* Last accessed January 15, 2018 from https:// www.facebook.com/TheOfficialGrumpyCat

180. Real Grumpy Cat. 2018. "About." *YouTube.com.* Last accessed January 15, 2018 from https://www. youtube.com/user/SevereAvoidance/about

181. News.com.au. 2014. "Ben Lashes is the meme manager behind Grumpy Cat, Keyboard Cat and Ridiculously Photogenic Guy." *News.com.au,* June 5. Last accessed January 10, 2018 from http://www. news.com.au/finance/business/media/ben-lashes-is-the-meme-manager-behind-grumpy-cat-keyboard-cat-and-ridiculously-photogenic-guy/news-story/ 5844c3ceaf6b77adfd4efc6198fdc444

182. O'Connor, Clare. 2017. "Forbes top influencers: Grumpy Cat, The Internet's Original Pet Superstar, Reigns Supreme." *Forbes,* September 26. Last accessed January 9, 2018 from https://www.forbes. com/sites/clareoconnor/2017/09/26/forbes-top-influencers-grumpy-cat-the-internets-original-pet-superstar-reigns-supreme/#f7b4a81287ad

183. Fleming Jr, Mike. 2013. "Grumpy Cat gets garfield-like movie deal." *Deadline.com,* May29. Last accessed January 15, 2018 from http://deadline.com/2013/05/if-this-doesnt-make-her-smile-nothing-will-grumpy-cat-gets-movie-deal-509211/

184. O'Connor, Clare. 2017. "Forbes top influencers: Grumpy Cat, The Internet's Original Pet Superstar, Reigns Supreme." *Forbes,* September 26. Last accessed January 9, 2018 from https://www.forbes.com/sites/clareoconnor/2017/09/26/forbes-top-influencers-grumpy-cat-the-internets-original-pet-superstar-reigns-supreme/#f7b4a81287ad

185. Walsh, Ben. 2014. "Report that Grumpy Cat earned $100 million is 'Completely Inaccurate'." *Huffington Post,* December 9. Last accessed January 15, 2018 from http://www.huffingtonpost.com.au/entry/grumpy-cat-100-million_n_6288502

186. O'Connor, Clare. 2017. "Forbes top influencers: Grumpy Cat, The Internet's Original Pet Superstar, Reigns Supreme." *Forbes,* September 26. Last accessed January 9, 2018 from https://www.forbes.com/sites/clareoconnor/2017/09/26/forbes-top-influencers-grumpy-cat-the-internets-original-pet-superstar-reigns-supreme/#f7b4a81287ad

187. BBC. 2015. "'Can't hide it forever': The model who became a meme." *BBC News,* October 29. Last accessed January 9, 2018 from http://www.bbc.com/news/world-asia-34568674

188. BBC. 2015. "'Can't hide it forever': The model who became a meme." *BBC News,* October 29. Last accessed January 9, 2018 from http://www.bbc.com/news/world-asia-34568674

189. Johnson, Sarah. 2012. "Chinese man sues his wife for being ugly, and the court AGREES... awarding

him £75,000." Daily Mail Australia, 27 October. Last accessed from 21 January 2018 from http://www.dailymail.co.uk/news/article-2223718/Chinese-man-sues-wife-ugly-court-AGREES--awarding-120-000.html

190. BBC. 2015. "'Can't hide it forever': The model who became a meme." *BBC News,* October 29. Last accessed January 9, 2018 from http://www.bbc.com/news/world-asia-34568674

191. BBC. 2015. "'Can't hide it forever': The model who became a meme." *BBC News,* October 29. Last accessed January 9, 2018 from http://www.bbc.com/news/world-asia-34568674

192. Milner, Ryan M. 2016. *The World Made Meme: Public Conversations and Participatory Media.* Cambridge, Massachusetts: MIT Press, p. 194.

193. Know Your Meme. 2018b. "Ugly children lawsuit hoax." *Knowyourmeme.com.* Last accessed January 9, 2018 from http://knowyourmeme.com/memes/ugly-children-lawsuit-hoax

194. Michelle Langer. 2013. "Kai singing Bruno Mars song Grenade." *YouTube.com,* February 26, 2013. Last accessed January 17, 2018 from https://www.youtube.com/watch?v=lKm12WlEigo

195. WNEP-TV. 2014. "'Apparently' this kid is awesome, steals the show during interview." *YouTube.com,* August 4, 2014. Last accessed January 17, 2018 from https://www.youtube.com/watch?v=rz5TGN7eUcM

196. Herrera, Monica. 2010. "Lady Gaga surprises 'Paparazzi' fan Greyson Chance on 'Ellen'." *Billboard,* May 13. Last accessed January 17, 2018 from https://www.billboard.com/articles/columns/

viral-videos/958261/lady-gaga-surprises-paparazzi-
fan-greyson-chance-on-ellen

197. Goldsmith, Belinda. 2010. "Ellen DeGeneres signs
Greyson Chance to new label." *Billboard,* May 26.
Last accessed January 17, 2018 from https://www.
billboard.com/articles/news/958057/ellen-degeneres-
signs-greyson-chance-to-new-label

198. Aniftos, Rania. 2017. "From YouTube covers
to originals, Greyson Chance's 6 best songs."
Billboard, December 8. Last accessed January 17,
2018 from https://www.billboard.com/articles/
columns/pop/8062645/greyson-chance-songs-best

199. Sophia Grace. 2011a. "Nicki Minaj – Super
Bass by Sophia Grace Brownlee | Sophia Grace."
YouTube.com, September 19, 2011. Last accessed
January 17, 2018 from https://www.youtube.com/
watch?v=C7hTAp6KrGY

200. TheEllenShow. 2011a. "Sophia Grace's show
stopping performance!" *YouTube.com,* October 12,
2011. Last accessed January 17, 2018 from https://
www.youtube.com/watch?v=odhUPMYXpX4

201. TheEllenShow. 2011b. "Nicki Minaj sings
'Super Bass' with Sophia Grace (Full Version)."
YouTube.com, October 12, 2011. Last accessed
January 17, 2018 from https://www.youtube.com/
watch?v=f9573kGBtuE

202. TheEllenShow. 2011c. "Sophia and Rosie dance
during break." *YouTube.com,* October 12, 2011.
Last accessed January 17, 2018 from https://www.
youtube.com/watch?v=RALcbuWaWE0

203. TheEllenShow. 2011d. "Sophia Grace and Rosie:
AMA correspondents!" *YouTube.com,* November 7,

2011. Last accessed January 17, 2018 from https://www.youtube.com/watch?v=JJB-Wx7l8A0

204. TheEllenShow. 2012a. "Exclusive: Sophia Grace & Rosie bonus VMA footage." *YouTube.com,* September 11, 2012. Last accessed January 17, 2018 from https://www.youtube.com/watch?v=zvoXMFNIcbg

205. TheEllenShow. 2013a. "Exclusive! Sophia Grace & Rosie bonus Grammy footage!" *YouTube.com,* February 11, 2013. Last accessed January 17, 2018 from https://www.youtube.com/watch?v=BpPpEJenhV8

206. TheEllenShow. 2012b. "Sophia Grace & Rosie love target." *YouTube.com,* May 10, 2012. Last accessed January 17, 2018 from https://www.youtube.com/watch?v=ar97Iu-5qh4

207. TheEllenShow. 2012c. "Sophia Grace & Rosie meet Fijit!" *YouTube.com,* October 2, 2012. Last accessed January 17, 2018 from https://www.youtube.com/watch?v=0-MsShNsKgY

208. TheEllenShow. 2013b. "Exclusive! Sophia Grace & Rosie meet the Disney Princesses." *YouTube.com,* May 16, 2013. Last accessed January 17, 2018 from https://www.youtube.com/watch?v=FzVk9-9XAow

209. TheEllenShow. 2013d. "'Tea Time' with Sophia Grace & Rosie." *YouTube.com,* May 31, 2013. Last accessed January 17, 2018 from https://www.youtube.com/watch?v=AUIep_UoKUc&list=PLuW4g7xujBWcaDNqBoQqlbXqBzXE5nyNA

210. TheEllenShow. 2012d. "Sophia Grace & Rosie have 100M views on YouTube!" *YouTube.*

com, April 25, 2012. Last accessed January 17, 2018 from https://www.youtube.com/watch?v=Aspr2r9km3Y

211. TheEllenShow. 2013c. "Sophia Grace & Rosie on their new book and movie!" *YouTube.com,* November 15, 2013. Last accessed January 17, 2018 from https://www.youtube.com/watch?v=zns6hZu6FRQ

212. TheEllenShow. 2014. "World premiere! Sophia Grace & Rosie's movie!" *YouTube.com,* March 17, 2014. Last accessed January 17, 2018 from https://www.youtube.com/watch?v=ZP8ZnAIwdA4

213. Sophia Grace. 2011b. *YouTube.com,* September 15, 2011. Last accessed January 17, 2018 from https://www.youtube.com/user/SophiaGraceBrownlee/about

214. SophiaGraceTheArtist. n.d. "Sophia Grace." *Facebook.com.* Last accessed January 17, 2018 from https://www.facebook.com/pg/SophiaGraceTheArtist/about/?ref=page_internal

215. Kimball, Trevor. 2018. "*Little Big Shots:* Season three premiere date announced by NBC." *TV Series Finale,* January 6. Last accessed January 17, 2018 from https://tvseriesfinale.com/tv-show/little-big-shots-season-three-premiere-date-announced-nbc/

216. Dubecki, Larissa. 2017. "Little Big Shots may be cute, but it's a long way from innocent, good fun." *Sydney Morning Herald,* August 31. Last accessed January 17, 2018 from http://www.smh.com.au/entertainment/tv-and-radio/little-big-shots-may-be-cute-but-its-a-long-way-from-innocent-good-fun-20170825-gy43lj.html

217. Lee, Yang Yi. 2017. "Celeb Tosh Zhang: YouTube gave me my break." *Smart Parents,* May 16. Last accessed January 17, 2018 from https://www.smartparents.sg/child/education/celeb-tosh-zhang-youtube-gave-me-my-break-8854000

218. The Straits Times. 2014. "The YouTube star next door." *The Straits Times,* April 14. Last accessed January 17, 2018 from http://www.straitstimes.com/lifestyle/entertainment/singaporean-youtube-stars-make-their-mark-online-and-offline

219. Eunice Annabel. 2014. "The Lion Men gala premiere!!!" *Euniceannabel.blogspot.com,* January 29. Last accessed January 17, 2018 from http://euniceannabel.blogspot.com.au/2014/01/the-lion-men-gala-premiere.html

220. Naomi Neo. 2013. "A day to remember." *Naomineo.squarespace.com,* March 15. Last accessed January 17, 2018 from https://naomi-neo.squarespace.com/?offset=1363718400000

221. Lingo Lingo Where You Go. 2014. "*CASTING CALL / AUDITIONS*." *Facebook.com,* October 31. Last accessed January 17, 2018 from https://www.facebook.com/LingoLingoWhereYouGo/posts/1493492100931212

222. Ng, Gwendolyn. 2016. "Singapore blogger Eunice Annabel Lim prefers acting after Gushcloud drama." *Her World,* January 5. Last accessed January 17, 2018 from http://www.herworld.com/celebs-men-sex/celebs/singapore-blogger-eunice-annabel-lim-acting-gushcloud-drama

223. MunahHirziOfficial. 2008. "MunahHirziOfficial." Last accessed January 18, 2018 from https://www.youtube.com/user/MunahHirziOfficial/about

224. Malinda-White, Kyle. 2012. "Munah & Hirzi are moving over to the television screen and they're ecstatic." *Popspoken,* October 16. Last accessed January 18, 2018 from http://popspoken.com/screen/2012/10/munah-hirzi-are-moving-over-to-the-television-screen-and-theyre-ecstatic

225. Malinda-White, Kyle. 2012. "Munah & Hirzi are moving over to the television screen and they're ecstatic." *Popspoken,* October 16. Last accessed January 18, 2018 from http://popspoken.com/screen/2012/10/munah-hirzi-are-moving-over-to-the-television-screen-and-theyre-ecstatic

226. Malinda-White, Kyle. 2012. "Munah & Hirzi are moving over to the television screen and they're ecstatic." *Popspoken,* October 16. Last accessed January 18, 2018 from http://popspoken.com/screen/2012/10/munah-hirzi-are-moving-over-to-the-television-screen-and-theyre-ecstatic

227. Mediacorp Suria. 2012a. "#MunahHirzi Action! is premiering soon at 9pm tonight." *Mediacorp Suria Facebook Page*, October 17. Last accessed January 18, 2018 from https://www.facebook.com/MediacorpSuria/posts/10151172883852893

228. Mediacorp Suria. 2012b. "EXCLUSIVE FOOTAGE: #MunahHirzi: 10 ways to film a trailer!" *Mediacorp Suria Facebook Page,* October 11. Last accessed January 18, 2018 from https://www.facebook.com/MediacorpSuria/posts/535963753084116

229. Mediacorp Suria. 2012b. "EXCLUSIVE FOOTAGE: #MunahHirzi: 10 ways to film a trailer!" *Mediacorp Suria Facebook Page,* October 11. Last accessed

January 18, 2018 from https://www.facebook.com/
MediacorpSuria/posts/535963753084116

230. azliah. 2013. "Munah and Hirzi: The face of
Singapore's Gen Y?" *Yahoo! Lifestyle,* March 8.
Accessed April 23, 2017 from https://sg.style.yahoo.
com/blogs/singapore-showbiz/munah-hirzi-face-
singapore-gen-y-181118474.html

231. azliah. 2013. "Munah and Hirzi: The face of
Singapore's Gen Y?" *Yahoo! Lifestyle,* March 8.
Accessed April 23, 2017 from https://sg.style.yahoo.
com/blogs/singapore-showbiz/munah-hirzi-face-
singapore-gen-y-181118474.html

232. mrbrown. 2006a. "TODAY: S'poreans are fed, up
with progress!" *mrbrown.com,* July 3. Last accessed
January 17, 2018 from http://www.mrbrown.com/
blog/2006/07/today_sporeans_.html

233. Aglionby, John. 2006. "Express yourself." *The
Guardian,* July 12. Last accessed January 17, 2018
from https://www.theguardian.com/world/2006/
jul/11/worlddispatch

234. mrbrown. 2006b. "Letter from MICA: Distorting
the truth, mr brown?" *mrbrown.com,* 3 July.
Last accessed January 17, 2018 from http://www.
mrbrown.com/blog/2006/07/letter_from_mic.html

235. mrbrown. 2006c. "Regarding TODAY." *mrbrown.
com,* July 6. Last accessed January 17, 2018 from
http://www.mrbrown.com/blog/2006/07/regarding_
today.html

236. Aglionby, John. 2006. "Express yourself." *The
Guardian,* July 12. Last accessed January 17, 2018

from https://www.theguardian.com/world/2006/
jul/11/worlddispatch

237. Winkler, Rolfe, Jack Nicas, and Ben Fritz. 2017.
     "Disney severs ties with YouTube star PewDiePie
     after anti-Semitic posts." *The Wall Street Journal,*
     February 14. Last accessed January 18, 2018 from
     https://www.wsj.com/articles/disney-severs-ties-
     with-youtube-star-pewdiepie-after-anti-semitic-
     posts-1487034533

238. Berg, Madeline. 2016. "The Highest-Paid YouTube
     Stars 2016: PewDiePie remains No. 1 with
     $15 million." *Forbes,* December 6. Last accessed
     January 18, 2018 from https://www.forbes.com/
     sites/maddieberg/2016/12/05/the-highest-paid-
     youtube-stars-2016-pewdiepie-remains-no-1-with-
     15-million/#3df5e6377713

239. Chokshi, Niraj. 2017. "Disney drops PewDiePie
     and YouTube distances itself after reports of anti-
     Semitic videos." *The New York Times,* February
     14. Last accessed January 18, 2018 from https://
     www.nytimes.com/2017/02/14/business/pewdiepie-
     youtube-disney.html?_r=0

240. Markiplier. 2017. "RESPECT." *YouTube.
     com,* February 17. Last accessed January
     18, 2018 from https://www.youtube.com/
     watch?v=YBMkrXG8KMY

241. h3h3Productions. 2017. "Is PewDiePie a racist?"
     YouTube.com, February 14. Last accessed
     January 18, 2018 from https://www.youtube.com/
     watch?v=JLNSiFrS3n4

242. DeFranco, Philip. 2017. "MSM tried to destroy
     PewDiePie and OMG It just backfired! So
     ridiculous…" *YouTube.com,* February 16. Last

accessed January 18, 2018 from https://www.
youtube.com/watch?v=DtlDC1sZFSg

243. h3h3Productions. 2017. "Is PewDiePie a racist?"
YouTube.com, February 14. Last accessed
January 18, 2018 from https://www.youtube.com/
watch?v=JLNSiFrS3n4

244. DeFranco, Philip. 2017. "MSM tried to destroy
PewDiePie and OMG It just backfired! So
ridiculous..." *YouTube.com,* February 16. Last
accessed January 18, 2018 from https://www.
youtube.com/watch?v=DtlDC1sZFSg

245. Hallam, Jed. 2013. *The Social Media Manifesto.*
New York: Palgrave Macmillan.

246. Bhargava, Rohit. 2008. *Personality not Included:
Why Companies Lose their Authenticity – and How
Great Brands Get it Back.* New York: McGraw-Hill.

247. Schaefer, Mark. 2012. *Return on influence: The
Revolutionary Power of Klout, Social Scoring, and
Influence Marketing.* New York: McGraw-Hill.

248. Li, Jiatao, Anne Tsui, and Elizabeth Weldon. 2000.
*Management and Organizations in the Chinese
Context.* New York: Macmillan Press.

249. Dent, Fiona E., and Mike Brent. 2006. *Influencing:
Skills and Techniques for Business Success.* New
York: Palgrave Macmillan.

250. Solis, Brian. 2012. *The End of Business as Usual:
Rewire the Way You Work to Succeed in the
Consumer Revolution.* Hoboken, New Jersey: John
Wiley & Sons.

251. Abidin, Crystal, and Eric C. Thompson. 2012.
"Buymylife.com: Cyberfemininities and commercial

intimacy in blogshops." *Women's Studies International Forum* 35(6): 467–477.

252. Abidin, Crystal. 2017. "#familygoals: Family Influencers, calibrated amateurism, and justifying young digital labour." *Social Media + Society* 3(2): 1–15.

253. Abidin, Crystal. 2013. "Cyber-BFFs: Assessing women's 'Perceived Interconnectedness' in Singapore's commercial lifestyle blog industry." *Global Media Journal, Australian Edition* 7(1): 1–20.

254. Abidin, Crystal. 2017c. "Influencer extravaganza: A decade of commercial 'lifestyle' microcelebrities in Singapore." Pp. 158–168 in *Routledge Companion to Digital Ethnography,* edited by Larissa Hjorth, Heather Horst, Genevieve Bell, and Anne Galloway. London: Routledge.

255. Nuffnang. 2013. "What's happening @ Nuffnang?" *Nuffnang.* Last accessed April 30, 2013 from http://www.nuffnang.com.sg/

256. Gushcloud. 2013. "Something exciting is brewing." *Gushcloud.* Last accessed April 30, 2013 from http://gushcloud.com/

257. Abidin, Crystal. 2014. "#In$tagLam: Instagram as a repository of taste, a brimming marketplace, a war of eyeballs." Pp. 119–128 in *Mobile Media Making in the Age of Smartphones,* edited by Marsha Berry and Max Schleser. New York: Palgrave Pivot.

258. Ladyironchef. 2010. "The truth about this Singapore food blog." *Ladyironchef.com,* August 24. Last accessed January 21, 2018 from http://www.ladyironchef.com/2010/08/truth/

259. Xiaxue. 2010. "Everybody hates Bloggers." *Xiaxue. blogpost.sg,* August 26. Last accessed January 21, 2018 from http://xiaxue.blogspot.se/2010/08/everybody-hates-bloggers.html

260. Thomas, Sujin. 2018. "Dublin hotel owner bans all social media influencers after 'exposing' one for asking for free 5-night stay." *Business Insider,* January 19. Last accessed January 21, 2018 from http://www.businessinsider.com/dublin-hotel-bans-social-media-influencers-after-elle-darby-asks-for-free-stay-2018-1?r=US&IR=T&IR=T

261. buzzoid. 2016. "Buy Instagram Followers." *Buzzoid.com.* Last accessed December 5, 2016 from http://buzzoid.com/buy- instagram-followers/

262. igReviews. 2016. "Buy Instagram followers reviews." *Igreviews.org.* Last accessed December 5, 2016 from http://igreviews.org/

263. Lee, Dave. 2014. "Instagram deletes millions of accounts in spam purge." *BBC,* December 19. Last accessed January 21, 2018 from http://www.bbc.com/news/technology-30548463

264. TagBlender. 2018. "TagBlender offers the best way of promoting your Instagram account by using tags." *Tagblender.net.* Last accessed January 21, 2018 from http://www.tagblender.net/

265. Hashtags For Likes. 2018. "#Hashtags for likes." *Hashtagsforlikes.co.* Last accessed January 21, 2018 from https://www.hashtagsforlikes.co/

266. Armenti, Marissa. 2017. "The Shadow Ban: Are Influencers being ghosted?" *Influence,* June 15. Last accessed January 21, 2018 from https://influence.

bloglovin.com/the-shadow-ban-are-influencers-being-ghosted-effc9cb374d9

267. Instagram for Business. 2017. "We understand users have experienced issues with our hashtag search that caused post to not be surfaced." *Facebook. com*, February 28. Last accessed January 21, 2018 from https://m.facebook.com/instagramforbusiness/posts/1046447858817451

268. Hunt, Elle. 2016. "New algorithm-driven Instagram feed rolled out to the dismay of users." *The Guardian*, June 7. Last accessed January 21, 2018 from https://www.theguardian.com/technology/2016/jun/07/new-algorithm-driven-instagram-feed-rolled-out-to-the-dismay-of-users

269. Kamen, Matt. 2016. "Twitter's non-chronological timeline is now opt-out." *Wired*, March 17. Last accessed January 21, 2018 from http://www.wired.co.uk/article/twitter-non-chronological-timeline-how-to-opt-out

270. Biersdorfer, J. D. 2016. "Putting your Twitter feed back in chronological Oorder." *The New York Times*, March 21. Last accessed January 21, 2018 from https://www.nytimes.com/2016/03/22/technology/personaltech/putting-your-twitter-feed-back-in-chronological-order.html

271. Kircher, Madison Malone. 2016. "Election self-care tip: Turn off out-of-order sorting on social media." *New York Magazine*, November 9. Last accessed January 21, 2018 from http://nymag.com/selectall/2016/11/how-to-turn-off-algorithm-on-instagram-facebook-and-twitter.html

272. Thompson, Rachel. 2017. "The Instagram 'pods' using likes to fight the new algorithm." *Mashable*,

April 19. Last accessed January 21, 2018 from https://mashable.com/2017/04/19/instagram-pods-bloggers/#Wqme2Gm9viqm

273. Reinstein, Julia. 2018. "'Tweetdecking' is taking over Twitter. Here's everything you need to know." *Buzzfeed,* January 12. Last accessed January 21, 2018 from https://www.buzzfeed.com/juliareinstein/exclusive-networks-of-teens-are-making-thousands-of-dollars?utm_term=.ig3Vmae5YG#.fuDxMEQd0v

274. Reinstein, Julia. 2018. "'Tweetdecking' is taking over Twitter. Here's everything you need to know." *Buzzfeed,* January 12. Last accessed January 21, 2018 from https://www.buzzfeed.com/juliareinstein/exclusive-networks-of-teens-are-making-thousands-of-dollars?utm_term=.ig3Vmae5YG#.fuDxMEQd0v

275. Fearn, Rebecca. 2017. "Beauty blogger Huda Kattan tops Instagram rich list (& she earns a *LOT* per post)…" *Glamour,* June 30. Last accessed January 21, 2018 from http://www.glamourmagazine.co.uk/article/instagram-rich-list-2017

276. Noyan, Burcu. 2017. "Brands are relying on 'Influencer' marketing more than ever." *Fortune,* July 13. Last accessed January 21, 2018 from http://fortune.com/2017/07/13/brands-influencer-marketing-advertisement/

277. Govani, Shinan. 2017. "The mysterious world of social media influencers: Govani." *The Star,* July 11. Last accessed January 21, 2018 from https://www.thestar.com/entertainment/2017/07/11/under-the-influence-of-the-almost-famous-govani.html

278. Bradley, Diana. 2017a. "The not-so-secret weapon in cause marketing: Engaged influencers." *PR Week,* June 26. Last accessed January 21, 2018 from https://www.prweek.com/article/1437705/not-so-secret-weapon-cause-marketing-engaged-influencers

279. Smart Insights. 2017. "The rise and rise of Influencer marketing." *Smart Insights,* February 21. Last accessed January 21, 2018 from https://www.smartinsights.com/online-pr/influencer-marketing/rise-rise-influencer-marketing/

280. Warna, Emily. 2017. "The death of Influencer marketing?" *Art + Marketing,* March 14. Last accessed January 21, 2018 from https://artplusmarketing.com/the-death-of-influencer-marketing-c82338eff6eb

281. Perez, Sarah. 2017. "Amazon quietly launches its own social media influencer program into beta." *Tech Crunch,* March 31. Last accessed January 21, 2018 from https://techcrunch.com/2017/03/31/amazon-quietly-launches-its-own-social-media-influencer-program-into-beta/

282. Bernard, Zoë. 2017. "Billion-dollar lip-syncing app Musical.ly is passing out $50 million worth of grants to support its users." *Business Insider,* December 19. Last accessed January 21, 2018 from http://nordic.businessinsider.com/musically-launches-creator-fund-grants-2017-12?r=US&IR=T

283. Hallanan, Lauren. 2017. "Ruhan: Blogger incubators disrupt China's ecommerce industry." *Parklu,* September 14. Last accessed January 21, 2018 from http://www.parklu.com/ruhan-blogger-incubators-china-ecommerce/

284. Gontcharova, Natalie. 2017. "You can now go to college to become a social media star." *Refinery 29,* June 20. Last accessed January 21, 2018 from http://www.refinery29.com/2017/06/160004/social-media-influencer-class-china-university

285. Ellis, Jack. 2017. "Influencer marketing firm Gushcloud gets $3m from K-wave giant YG." *Tech in Asia,* October 16. Last accessed January 21, 2018 from https://www.techinasia.com/gushcloud-3m-yg-investment

286. PR Newswire. 2017. "GinzaMetrics to acquire Withfluence, Influencer marketing platform to create powerful content creation and amplification offering." *PR Newswire,* October 17. Last accessed January 21, 2018 from https://www.prnewswire.com/news-releases/ginzametrics-to-acquire-withfluence-influencer-marketing-platform-to-create-powerful-content-creation-and-amplification-offering-300538036.html

287. Bradley, Diana. 2017b. "Citizen relations acquires experiential, influencer shop: The narrative group." *PR Week,* September 20. Last accessed January 21, 2018 from https://www.prweek.com/article/1445208/citizen-relations-acquires-experiential-influencer-shop-narrative-group

288. Slefo, George. 2017. "Publishers snapped up marketing agencies at unprecedented rate in 2016." *Ad Age,* January 17. Last accessed January 21, 2018 from http://adage.com/article/digital/publishers-acquiring-marketing-agencies-surged-2016/307498/

289. Phan, Michelle. 2017. "Michelle Phan: Why I had to leave everything & start over." *Refinery 29,* June 2. Last accessed January 21, 2018 from http://www.

refinery29.com/2017/04/149365/michelle-phan-ipsy-em-cosmetics-relaunch

290. McLaughlin, Erin. 2017. "'On Fleek' inventor Kayla Newman AKA Peaches Monroe on her beauty line." *Teen Vogue,* March 9. Last accessed January 21, 2018 from https://www.teenvogue.com/story/on-fleek-inventor-kayla-newman-aka-peaches-monroe-on-her-beauty-line

291. Business of Fashion. 2017. "Chiara Ferragni Opens Milan Boutique, Gabi Gregg and Nicolette Mason's New Brand." *Business of Fashion,* July 24. Last accessed January 21, 2018 from https://www.businessoffashion.com/articles/news-bites/gabi-gregg-nicolette-mason-premme-chiara-ferragni-milan-boutique

292. Barker, Christian. 2017. "Macau-born social media influencer-turned-designer Yoyo Cao at Singapore Fashion Week." *South China Morning Post,* October 31. Last accessed January 21, 2018 from http://www.scmp.com/lifestyle/fashion-luxury/article/2117732/macau-born-social-media-influencer-turned-designer-yoyo-cao

293. Purtill, James. 2017a. "Instafamous must reveal #ads under new transparency rules." *ABC,* March 1. Last accessed January 21, 2018 from http://www.abc.net.au/triplej/programs/hack/social-influencers-must-reveal-ad-under-new-transparency-rules/8315962

294. Hunt, Elle. 2017. "Social media stars face crackdown over money from brands." *The Guardian,* September 16. Last accessed January 21, 2018 from https://www.theguardian.com/technology/2017/sep/16/social-media-stars-face-crackdown-over-money-from-brands

295. Fortune. 2017. "Instagram 'Influencers' are being forced to disclose endorsement deals." *Fortune,* September 14. Last accessed January 21, 2018 from http://fortune.com/2017/09/13/instagram-influencers-endorsement-deals/

296. Boboltz, Sara. 2017. "More people are now suing Fyre festival for obvious reasons." *Huffington Post,* May 3. Last accessed January 21, 2018 from http://www.huffingtonpost.com.au/entry/fyre-festival-second-lawsuit_us_59099029e4b02655f8423485

297. Stern, Carly. 2017. "Those coveted blue check marks don't come cheap!" *Dailymail,* September 14. Last accessed January 21, 2018 from http://www.dailymail.co.uk/femail/article-4885188/There-s-BLACK-MARKET-getting-verified-Instagram.html

298. Nord, James. 2017. "Cheaters never prosper – not even in social media." *Forbes,* September 25. Last accessed January 21, 2018 from https://www.forbes.com/sites/forbesagencycouncil/2017/09/25/cheaters-never-prosper-not-even-in-social-media/#561a30036cf9

299. Purtill, James. 2017b. "InstaFraud: How fake Instagram 'influencers' are gaming brands for money." *ABC,* August 18. Last accessed January 21, 2018 from http://www.abc.net.au/triplej/programs/hack/how-fake-instagram-influencers-are-gaming-brands-for-money/8821440

300. Wallace, Francesca. 2017. "Street style photographers aren't happy with your favourite influencers, a battle is brewing." *Vogue,* September 25. Last accessed January 21, 2018 from https://www.vogue.com.au/fashion/news/street-style-photographers-arent-happy-with-your-favourite-influencers-a-battle-is-brewing/news-story/8493a5154ad6d80a0fe1822b09b37ff1

301. Ellis, Emma Grey. 2017. "Everyone loses when your employer owns your Facebook account." *Wired,* May 4. Last accessed January 21, 2018 from https://www.wired.com/2017/04/tomi-lahren-the-blaze-sock-puppet/

302. BBC. 2017. "Singapore teen blogger Amos Yee granted US asylum." *BBC,* March 25. Last accessed January 21, 2018 from http://www.bbc.com/news/world-us-canada-39388810

303. Leaver, Tama, and Crystal Abidin. 2017. "When exploiting kids for cash goes wrong on YouTube: The lessons of DaddyOFive." *The Conversation,* May 2. Last accessed January 21, 2018 from https://theconversation.com/when-exploiting-kids-for-cash-goes-wrong-on-youtube-the-lessons-of-daddyofive-76932

304. Tantiangco, Aya. 2017. "Pinay Instagram model apologizes after 'racist' tweets from 2013 surface." *GMA News Online,* May 5. Last accessed January 21, 2018 from http://www.gmanetwork.com/news/hashtag/content/609647/pinay-instagram-model-apologizes-after-racist-tweets-from-2013-surface/story/

305. Tan, Guan Zhen, and Nyi Nyi Thet. 2017. "S'pore YouTuber's makeup video somehow leads to an intense discussion on race." *Mothership,* April 27. Last accessed January 21, 2018 from https://mothership.sg/2017/04/spore-youtubers-makeup-video-somehow-leads-to-an-intense-discussion-on-race/

306. Yu, Heather Johnson. 2017. "Twitch Streamer cyberbullied by racist bros after posting photo of Asian boyfriend." *Next Shark,* October 30. Last accessed January 21, 2018 from https://nextshark.com/pink-sparkles-twitch-streamer-drinks-the-salty-tears-of-racist-bros-after-posting-photo-of-asian-boyfriend/

307. Herreria, Carla. 2017. "Blogger praises K-Beauty while calling Asians 'Ching Chongs' in 'Funny Clothes'." *Huffington Post,* July 20. Last accessed January 21, 2018 from https://www.huffingtonpost.com/entry/cocomadkilla-ching-chong-korean-review_us_59713eece4b0e79ec19840fd

308. Kircher, Madison Malone. 2017a. "A conversation with YouTube's favorite 10-year-old communist Vlogger." *New York Magazine,* February 21. Last accessed January 21, 2018 from http://nymag.com/selectall/2017/02/youtubes-best-vlogger-is-a-10-year-old-communist.html

309. Wallace, Julia. 2017. "Cambodia's Buddhist monks find a second calling: Political correspondent." *The New York Times,* June 4. Last accessed January 21, 2018 from https://www.nytimes.com/2017/06/04/world/asia/cambodia-elections-buddhist-monks.html

310. Miller, Joshua Rhett. 2017. "This young mom is the face of Mormonism's hateful alt-right." *New York Post,* March 31. Last accessed January 21, 2018 from https://nypost.com/2017/03/31/this-young-mom-is-the-face-of-mormonisms-hateful-alt-right/

311. Farokhmanesh, Megan. 2017. "The Bow Wow challenge is a hilarious reminder that everyone lies on social media." *The Verge,* May 10. Last accessed January 21, 2018 from https://www.theverge.com/2017/5/10/15612724/bow-wow-challenge-social-media-lies

312. Cowie, Tom. 2017. "Belle Gibson fined $410,000 after misleading people with claims she cured cancer." *Sydney Morning Herald,* September 28. Last accessed January 21, 2018 from http://www.smh.com.au/business/consumer-affairs/belle-gibson-

fined-410000-after-misleading-people-with-claims-
she-cured-cancer-20170927-gyq86z.html

313. Tait, Amelia. 2017. "Why are children on YouTube
saying their parents are dead?" *NewStatesman,*
March 14. Last accessed January 21, 2018 from
https://www.newstatesman.com/science-tech/
internet/2017/03/why-are-children-youtube-saying-
their-parents-are-dead

314. Sales, Nancy Jo. 2017. "First she became a 13-year-
old internet meme. Now, she's treated like a porn
star." *The Guardian,* March 23. Last accessed
January 21, 2018 from https://www.theguardian.
com/commentisfree/2017/mar/23/sexualization-13-
year-old-internet-meme-cash-me-ousside

315. Pressly, Linda. 2017. "Cam-girls: Inside the
Romanian sexcam industry." *BBC,* August 10. Last
accessed January 21, 2018 from http://www.bbc.
com/news/magazine-40829230

316. Liew, Isabelle. 2017. "Ngee Ann Poly makes police
report over blog targeting students." *The New
Paper,* June 16. Last accessed January 21, 2018
from http://www.tnp.sg/news/singapore/ngee-ann-
poly-makes-police-report-over-blog-targeting-
students

317. Chu, Kathy, and Menglin Huang. 2017. "How
a toddler who loves eating transfixed China."
The Wall Street Journal, May 21. Last accessed
January 21, 2018 from https://www.wsj.com/
articles/how-a-toddler-who-loves-eating-transfixed-
china-1495387268

318. Schmidt, Samantha. 2017. "6-year-old made
$11 million in one year reviewing toys on

YouTube." *The Washington Post,* December 11. Last accessed January 21, 2018 from https://www.washingtonpost.com/news/morning-mix/wp/2017/12/11/6-year-old-made-11-million-in-one-year-reviewing-toys-on-you-tube/?utm_term=.616913ad5930

319. Vice. 2017. "Meet Coco, the six-year-old Instagram star." *Vice,* August 22. Last accessed January 21, 2018 from https://broadly.vice.com/en_us/article/qvvzdm/meet-coco-the-six-year-old-instagram-star

320. Malleta, King. 2017. "YouTube pioneer KevJumba rises from the dead, gives insight to why he left YouTube." *Nextshark,* March 28. Last accessed January 21, 2018 from https://nextshark.com/kevjumba-rises-from-dead/

321. Makalintal, Bettina. 2017. "Why watching people break up on YouTube is so addictive." *The Atlantic,* April 3. Last accessed January 21, 2018 from https://www.theatlantic.com/technology/archive/2017/04/when-youtube-stars-breakup/521727/

322. General, Ryan. 2017. "Ryan Higa and friends create K-Pop group as a joke, gets #1 hit on K-Pop charts." *Nextshark,* March 27. Last accessed January 21, 2018 from https://nextshark.com/ryan-higa-kpop-parody-itunes-chart/

323. Newton, Casey. 2017. "Instagram is pushing restaurants to be kitschy, colorful, and irresistible to photographers." *The Verge,* July 20. Last accessed January 21, 2018 from https://www.theverge.com/2017/7/20/16000552/instagram-restaurant-interior-design-photo-friendly-media-noche

324. Wiener, Anna. 2017. "The Millennial Walt Disney."
     New York Magazine, October 4. Last accessed January
     21, 2018 from http://nymag.com/selectall/2017/10/
     museum-of-ice-cream-maryellis-bunn.html

325. Instagram. 2016. "Introducing Instagram stories."
     Instagram.com, August 2. Last accessed January
     21, 2018 from http://blog.instagram.com/
     post/148348940287/160802-stories

326. Abidin, Crystal. 2016. "Aren't these just young, rich
     women doing vain things online?: Influencer selfies
     as subversive frivolity." *Social Media + Society* 2(2):
     1–17.

327. Constine, Josh. 2016. "Instagram CEO on stories:
     Snapchat deserves all the credit." *Tech Crunch,*
     August 2. Last accessed January 21, 2018 from
     https://techcrunch.com/2016/08/02/silicon-copy/

328. Abidin, Crystal. 2014. "#In$tagLam: Instagram as a
     repository of taste, a brimming marketplace, a war
     of eyeballs." Pp. 119–128 in *Mobile Media Making
     in the Age of Smartphones,* edited by Marsha Berry
     and Max Schleser. New York: Palgrave Pivot.

329. Abidin, Crystal. 2017b. "Vote for my selfie:
     Politician selfies as charismatic engagement."
     Pp. 75–87 in *Selfie Citizenship*, edited by Adi
     Kuntsman. London: Palgrave Pivot.

330. Kircher, Madison Malone. 2017b. "Instagram really,
     really wants you to create a second account." *New
     York Magazine,* May 5. Last accessed January 21,
     2018 from http://nymag.com/selectall/2017/05/
     instagram-wants-users-to-make-second-finstagram-
     accounts.html

331. Abidin, Crystal. 2016. "Aren't these just young, rich women doing vain things online?: Influencer selfies as subversive frivolity." *Social Media + Society* 2(2): 1–17.

332. Roberts, Kevin. 2005. *Lovemarks: The Future Beyond Brands.* Brooklyn: Powerhouse Books.

333. Twitter. 2015. "Hearts on Twitter." *Twitter.com,* November 3. Last accessed January 21, 2018 from https://blog.twitter.com/official/en_us/a/2015/hearts-on-twitter.html

334. Kozinets, Robert V., Kristine de Valck, Andrea V. Wojnicki, and Sarah J. S. Wilner. 2010. "Networked narratives: Understanding word-of-mouth marketing in online communities." *American Marketing Association* 74: 71–89.

FURTHER READING

MILESTONE WORKS TOWARD INTERNET CELEBRITY

Internet celebrities are certainly not a new phenomenon and have been studied in various iterations in the last decade. For instance, as vocational internet celebrities, Influencers in Singapore root their earliest beginnings in blogshop culture in the mid-2000s (see Chapter 4). Considering the rich history and thematic contexts of internet celebrity, this section briefly introduces five epochs of milestone academic research on digital media, that provides the backdrop for the rise of internet celebrity.

Digital Platforms + Content Creation

The first epoch considers digital platforms in relation to content creation. The texts include major studies of the structural, economic, social, and cultural histories of various self-publishing and social media formats. Concerning blogging, key texts include cultural studies scholar Aaron Barlow's *The Rise of the Blogosphere* (2007), professor of English and biographer Mary Cross's *Bloggerati, Twitterati* (2011), and digital culture scholar Jill Walker Rettberg's *Blogging* (2013). Concerning social network, key texts include anthropologist Daniel Miller's *Tales from Facebook* (2011), communication scholar

Adrienne Massanari's study of Reddit in *Participatory Culture, Community, and Play* (2015), and journalism and sociology scholar Dhiraj Murthy's *Twitter* (2018). Concerning content-sharing sites for audio-visual media, key texts include digital media scholars Jean Burgess's and Joshua Green's *YouTube* (2013), and communication scholar Patrik Wikström's *The Music Industry* (2013). Although these texts do not focus on internet celebrities per se, they crucially outline how these digital platforms come into being and the nature of users' relationships with content consumption and production.

Barlow, Aaron. 2007. *The Rise of the Blogosphere.* Santa Barbara, CA: Praeger.

Cross, Mary. 2011. *Bloggerati, Twitterati: How Blogs and Twitter are Transforming Popular Culture.* Santa Barbara, CA: Praeger.

Massanari, Adrienne. 2015. *Participatory Culture, Community, and Play: Learning from Reddit.* Bern: Peter Lang.

Miller, Daniel. 2011. *Tales from Facebook.* Cambridge: Polity Press.

Murthy, Dhiraj. 2018. *Twitter: Social Communication in the Twitter Age.* Cambridge: Polity Press.

Rettberg, Jill Walker. 2013. *Blogging.* Cambridge: Polity Press.

Wikström, Patrik. 2013. *The Music Industry: Music in the Cloud.* Cambridge: Polity Press.

Digital Tools + Self-Branding

The second epoch considers digital tools in relation to self-branding. As iterated in the theoretical history of internet celebrity above, the origins of self-branding on the internet, pertaining to hobbyist histories of bedroom webcamming or networking users in Silicon Valley, highlight the use of digital media tools such as videocams, websites, and geo-location apps for users to construct a public persona. Major works include media studies scholar Theresa Senft's *Camgirls* (2008), which focused on how the webcam as a device became one of the first instruments to enable bedroom streaming as a hobby in the US, and how this has evolved to be taken up by various forms of trade including art and sex work; and communication scholar Alice Marwick's *Status Update* (2013), which studied the use of microcelebrity strategies among tech entrepreneurs managing startups in San Francisco to demonstrate how social media and microcelebrity techniques were used to complement traditional employment as a networking tool.

Marwick, Alice. 2013. *Status Update: Celebrity, Publicity and Branding in the Social Media Age.* New Haven, CT: Yale University Press.

Senft, Theresa M. 2008. *Camgirls: Celebrity and Community in the Age of Social Networks.* New York, NY: Peter Lang Publishers.

Blogging + Fashion

The third epoch considers blogging in relation to fashion. The first group of texts comprises fashion studies scholar Elizabeth Wissinger's *This Year's Model* (2015), anthropologist Brent Luvaas's *Street Style* (2016), and communication scholar Brooke Erin Duffy's *(Not) Getting Paid to Do What You Love* (2017). Collectively, they touch on microcelebrity as a practice, but have studied it specifically in the fashion industry in the American context. All texts look at how young people in the fashion industry use media as platforms to affiliate with corporations and fashion labels and sell themselves through forms of feminized labor such as "glamour labor" and "aspirational work." While Wissinger focuses more on traditional media formats like magazines, Duffy focuses on websites and blogs, while Luvaas focuses on photography. Many of these actors are known as "fashion bloggers," who form just one subset of internet celebrity in the industry. The second group of texts comprises anthropologist Brent Luvaas's *DIY Style* (2012), interdisciplinary scholar Minh-Ha T. Pham's *Asians Wear Clothes on the Internet* (2015), and art historian Reina Lewis's *Muslim Fashion* (2015). Collectively, they focus on fashion blogging as a hobby and source of income and have studied it specifically in the fashion industry comprising Asians. All texts look at how young people are using DIY publishing tools such as blogs to produce and curate digital content related to everyday fashion, and how the blogs produced by individuals come together to demonstrate collective cultural identities about the bloggers. Pham focuses on how race and gender are coded into the taste work of elite Asian bloggers in tandem with the Americentric fashion blogging ecology, Lewis looks at how young Muslim women are engaging in modest fashion in Britain, North America, and Turkey, and Luvaas focuses on a comparative analysis between DIY culture in Indonesia and Europe/the U.S. These texts and the people they study focus exclusively on fashion as a form of digital labor and content.

Duffy, Brooke Erin. 2017. *(Not) Getting Paid to Do What You Love: Gender, Social Media, and Aspirational Work*. New Haven, CT: Yale University Press.

Lewis, Reina. 2015. *Muslim Fashion: Contemporary Style Cultures*. Durham, NC: Duke University Press.

Luvaas, Brent. 2012. *DIY Style: Fashion, Music and Global Digital Cultures*. Cambridge: Bloomsbury.

Luvaas, Brent. 2016. *Street Style: An Ethnography of Fashion Blogging*. Cambridge: Bloomsbury.

Pham, Minh-Ha T. 2015. *Asians Wear Clothes on the Internet: Race, Gender, and the Work of Personal Style Blogging*. Durham, NC: Duke University Press.

Wissinger, Elizabeth. 2015. *This Year's Model: Fashion, Media, and the Making of Glamour*. New York, NY: NYU Press.

Internet-Native Formats + User Norms

The fourth epoch considers internet-native formats in relation to user norms. The texts include communication scholar Limor Shifman's *Memes in Digital Culture* (2013), information studies scholars Karine Nahon's and Jeff Hemsley's *Going Viral* (2013), media folklorist Whitney Phillips's *This Is Why We Can't Have Nice Things* (2015), communication scholar Ryan Milner's *The World Made Meme* (2016), digital media scholar Tim Highfield's *Social Media and Everyday Politics* (2016), and Phillips's and Milner's *The Ambivalent Internet* (2017). Collectively, the texts trace the rise of new internet media such as memes, hashtags, GIFs, and viral media on various social media platforms, and highlight how different communicative forms are variously adopted by disparate communities, sometimes branching off into subcultures requiring an extensive tacit knowledge of innuendos, double-speaking, code-switching, and cyclic referencing.

Highfield, Tim. 2016. *Social Media and Everyday Politics*. Cambridge: Polity Press.

Milner, Ryan M. 2016. The World Made Meme: Public Conversations and Participatory Media. Cambridge: MIT Press.

Nahon, Karine, and Jeff Hemsley. 2013. *Going Viral.* Cambridge: Polity Press.

Phillips, Whitney. 2015. *This Is Why We Can't Have Nice Things: Mapping the Relationship between Online Trolling and Mainstream Culture.* Cambridge, MA: MIT Press.

Phillips, Whitney, and Ryan M. Milner. 2017. *The Ambivalent Internet: Mischief, Oddity, and Antagonism Online.* Cambridge: Polity Press.

Shifman, Limor. 2013. *Memes in Digital Culture.* Cambridge, MA: MIT Press.

Internet Celebrity + Culture

The fifth epoch considers internet celebrity in relation to culture. Unlike texts of the first epoch that focused on platforms, texts of the second epoch that focused on techniques of self-branding, texts of the third epoch that focused on desktop publishing and the evolution of self-branded identity and entrepreneurship, and the fourth epoch that focused on emergent user norms across innovative internet-native formats, this new epoch considers the conditions and cultures of being a celebrity on the internet. Where media studies scholars Stuart Cunningham's and David Craig's *Social Media Entertainment* (forthcoming) focuses on the industry culture of content creators primarily on YouTube, the book you are reading focuses on the social and cultural aspects of what it means to have fame online.

Cunningham, Stuart, and David Craig. Forthcoming. *Social Media Entertainment: The New Industry at the Intersection of Hollywood and Silicon Valley.* New York, NY: NYU Press.

INDEX

NOTE: Page numbers followed by 'n' refers to endnotes.